Lei

MW00912209

MONTREAL
Get Around Town!™
52 Fun Things to Do
Right Here in Montreal

NO FIXED ADDRESS PUBLICATIONS

Get Around Town! Montreal
52 Fun Things to Do Right Here in Montreal
1st edition

Published by
No Fixed Address Publications, P.O. Box 65, NDG Station, Montreal, Quebec,
H4A 3P4, Canada
e-mail: nfa@cam.org

Writing: Leif R. Montin
Editing: Karin Montin
Research: Sophie Dupré
Maps: Kate McDonnell
Design and Layout: Irma Mazzonna
Additional Icons: John Custy
Photos: Leif R. Montin / No Fixed Address Publications (except where indicated)
Photo of the Author: Owen Egan

Cover Photos:
Place Jacques Cartier (photo: Stéphane Poulin)
Mille Îles River Regional Park
Circuit 500

Canadian Distribution (English version):
Hushion House, 36 Northline Road, Toronto, Ontario, M4B 3E2, Canada
Tel: (416) 285-6100 Fax: (416) 285-1777

Canadian Distribution (French version):
J.D.M. Géo Distribution Inc., 5790 Donahue, Saint-Laurent, Québec, H4S 1C1 Canada
Tél.: (514) 956-8505; téléc.: (514) 956-9398

Canadian Cataloguing in Publication Data

Montin, Leif R., 1963-
    Get around town!, Montreal : 52 fun things to do right here in Montreal

Includes index.
ISBN 0-9681732-2-5

    1- Montréal (Quebec)—Guidebooks. 2. Montréal Region (Quebec)—Guidebooks. 3. Amuse-
ments—Quebec (Province)—Montréal—Guidebooks. 4. Amusements—Quebec (Province)—Montreal
Region—Guidebooks. I. Title.

FC2947.18.M554 1999   917.14'28044   C99-900994-X   F1054.5.M83M554 1999

Printed in Canada

Montreal and Surrounding Area

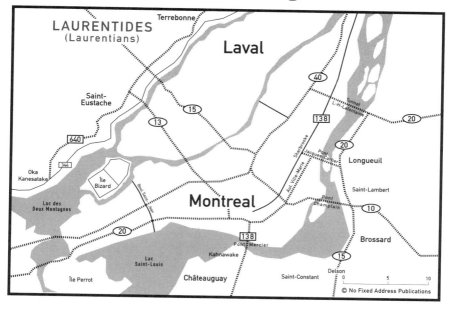

*With many thanks
to Pierre-Yves for his invaluable advice.*

*I would also like to thank Patrice Poissant, Rosalyne Hébert,
Pierre Tugas and Gilles Bengle for all their help.*

Contents

Symbols used

 Birdwatching

 Calendar Event

 Canoes

 Caving

 Cross-Country Skiing

 Cycling/Mountain Biking

 Dogs Welcome

 Farm Animals

 Fishing

 Free Admission

 Gift Shop/Boutique

 Hiking/Walking

 Historic Site

 Inline Skating

 Kayaks

 Museum

 Picnicking

 Pedalboats

 Rainy Day

 Restaurant

 Romantic Destination

 Rowboats

 Science Centre

 Skating

 Something Special for Children

 Snack Bar

 Snowshoeing

 Swimming

 Tobogganing

 Trains

 Volleyball

 Waterslides

 Wheelchair Accessible

 Wildlife Observation

Welcome
to Montreal!

Montreal is a terrific city with lots to see and do. And the best way to get to know it is by going out and seeing it! That's what this guide is all about. Cycling, picnicking, discovering a new park or museum ... whatever the weather, whatever the season.

What better way to learn about the city's rich history than by strolling the cobblestone streets of Old Montreal or taking in the view from the top of Mount Royal? But history is not the only thing to discover.

Explore outer space or examine insects, tour a recycling facility or look at model trains. There are scientific and technical activities galore.

The natural world beckons, as well. Whether you want to paddle a canoe, visit a farm, cycle through some pristine woods or simply have a picnic by the river, you can do it in and around Montreal.

• Looking for something to do? Flip through the pages until something catches your eye. A quick glance at the margin will tell you what the destination is all about, including if it's good for a rainy day.

• Have a specific idea in mind? Don't forget the index. Entries under activities such as swimming, cross-country skiing and karting will put you on the right track.

So what are you waiting for? Get Around Town!

Central Montreal

Montreal is a city made for walking, and nowhere is this truer than in the downtown core. Built in the days before the proliferation of cars, it is still best toured on foot: Ste Catherine, with the major stores and cinemas ... upscale Crescent and Bishop streets ... multicultural St Lawrence (a.k.a. the Main) ... and chic St Denis.

✪ In each of these areas, past and present are neatly juxtaposed. Modern constructions seem right at home next to turn-of-the-century greystone manors. It's a cultural blend, too, with business people and

artists mixing in the cafés and bars. ✿ This section describes a variety of urban attractions, from a tour of the stock exchange to a "lunchtime cruise" in a restaurant modelled after an ocean liner. It also presents a few ideas that don't have a fixed address. Heritage Montreal, for example, offers walking tours of neighbourhoods throughout the city. And if you want to get off the island, but don't have a car, you'll be  interested in the clubs that lead day trips into the countryside. ✿ For a list of other noteworthy places not covered by the articles, see the "Quick Guide to Major Attractions" on page 146.

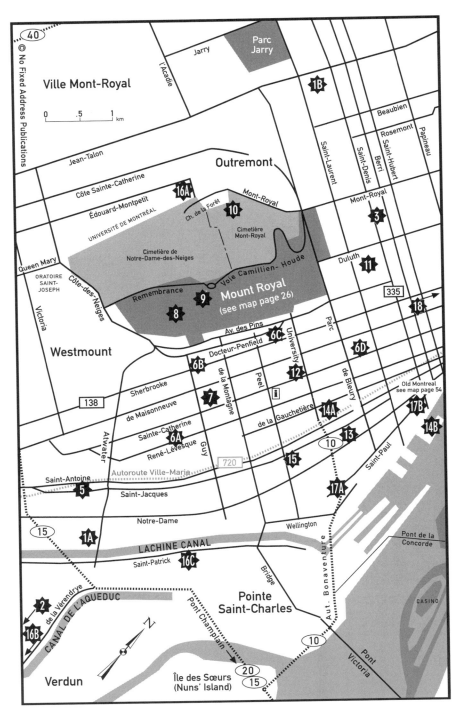

TRIP DESTINATIONS
(denoted by star symbol on map)

1A. Atwater Market
138 Atwater Ave
(514) 937-7754
p. 12

1B. Jean Talon Market
7075 Casgrain
(514) 277-1588
p. 12

2. Aquadome
1411 Lapierre St.
(514) 367-6460
p. 14

3. Ceramic Café
4201B St Denis
(514) 848-1119
p. 16

5. Émile Berliner Sound Wave Museum
1050 Lacasse, suite C-220
(514) 932-9663
p. 20

6A. Canadian Centre for Architecture
1920 Baile
(514) 939-7026
p. 22

6B. Montreal Museum of Fine Arts
1379 Sherbrooke West
(514) 285-1600
p. 22

6C. Redpath Museum
859 Sherbrooke West
(514) 398-4086, ext. 4092
p. 22

6D. Musée d'Art Contemporain
185 Ste Catherine West
(514) 847-6253
p. 22

7. Heritage Montreal
2180 Crescent
(514) 286-2662
p. 24

8. Mount Royal Park
(514) 872-6559
p. 28

9. Smith House
1260 Remembrance Rd
(514) 843-8240
p. 30

10. Mount Royal Cemetery
1297 Forest Rd
(514) 279-7358
p. 32

11. Colonial Baths
3963 Coloniale Ave.
(514) 285-0132
p. 34

12. Eaton's le 9ième
677 Ste Catherine West
(514) 284-8421
p. 36

13. Stock Exchange
800 Victoria Square
(514) 871-3582
p. 38

14A. Bell Amphitheatre (Skating)
1000 de la Gauchetière West
(514) 395-0555
p. 40

14B. Bonsecours Basin Old Port
(514) 282-5256
p. 40

15. Planetarium
1000 St Jacques West
(514) 872-4530
p. 42

16A. University of Montreal CEPSUM
2100 Édouard Montpetit
(514) 343-6150, 343-6993
p. 44

16B. André Laurendeau College
1111 Lapierre St
(514) 364-3320, ext. 249
p. 44

16C. Allez-Up Indoor Rock Climbing
1339 Shearer
(514) 989-9656
p. 44

17A. Montreal Railroad Modelers' Association
891 St Paul West
(514) 861-6185
p. 46

17B. Montreal Model Train Exhibition
350 St Paul East
(450) 659-9745 or
(514) 872-7730
p. 46

18. Ecomusée du Fier Monde
2050 Amherst
(514) 528-8444
p. 48

TOURIST INFORMATION

Tourism Quebec Infotourist Centre
1001 Dorchester Square
(514) 873-2015,
(800) 363-7777

Greater Montreal Convention and Tourism Bureau
1555 Peel
(514) 844-5000

Montreal Urban Community Transit Corporation (MUCTC)
(514) AUTO-BUS (288-6287)

Montreal's Fab Three
Outdoor Markets

A h, the excitement of market day. Jostling in the aisles, shamelessly touching, smelling, even tasting the produce before you buy. Filling the senses and whetting the appetite. In our city known for its rich culinary heritage, the markets are the source of farm-fresh locally grown fruits and vegetables, prized for their quality and flavour, and exotic treats from foreign ports, too.

Jean Talon Market is the biggest and most diverse of Montreal's three main outdoor markets—and is notoriously difficult for newcomers to locate. Tucked away behind very ordinary storefronts in Montreal's Italian district, it's worth the pavement pounding and head scratching, since there's nothing else like it in the city. You'll find all the sights and sounds you'd expect at a traditional market boasting over 250 stalls. Three long covered aisles are packed with merchants displaying fruit and vegetables, flowers and baked goods. Delicatessens and café-restaurants with small patios flank the square. This market is active in winter, too, when 25 stalls move to the central enclosed area.

Backing onto the Lachine Canal and linked to the bike path by a footbridge, the **Atwater Market** is, architecturally speaking, the grandest of all—its long, high golden brick building is framed on three sides by a covered promenade and topped by a distinctive tower. Built in 1933, it houses 30 shops and the administration offices for all the public markets. Surprisingly, there is also a gymnasium inside. Used in bygone days by boxing clubs, it now offers gymnastics lessons.

This market has gained a reputation among yuppies who like fresh produce and don't mind paying the price. Weekend mornings the parking lots are full and the aisles crowded, with line-ups at the excellent bakery-café. People flock to Atwater Market for good reason: it has a range of speciality food stores including a pasta shop, bulk-food store and well-stocked liquor store (with extended hours), plus a dozen butcher shops and *three* cheese shops, not to mention many outdoor stalls from March to October.

The **Maisonneuve Market**, on a gorgeous square just south of the Olympic Stadium, is the most recent addition to the fold, having reopened in 1995. This mainly indoor market is unmistakably modern, as light and airy as Vancouver's famous Granville Island market, though not nearly as big. The old Maisonneuve Market sits just to the side, an enormous granite edifice built in 1912. Once it was the city's most popular market, with over 2,000 patrons a day. It now serves as Hochelaga-Maisonneuve's community cultural centre.

The produce at all the markets varies seasonally. In March the markets herald the spring (and return of the outdoor stalls) with maple taffy on snow; in April petting zoos make an appearance at Jean Talon and Maisonneuve, painted eggs and live chicks at Atwater. May sees all three decked out with flowers ready for planting, while July is the month for Quebec-grown strawberries. In August a harvest festival pays tribute to selected Quebec specialties; mountains of pumpkins and squash arrive in October, and the year ends with Christmas tree sales in December.

Season and Hours
8 a.m.–6 p.m. Mon–Wed and Sat, 8 a.m.–9 p.m. Thur–Fri, 8 a.m.–5 p.m. Sun. Closed Christmas Day and New Year's Day.

JEAN TALON MARKET
7075 Casgrain (south of Jean Talon St)
(514) 277-1588
Directions
Orange or Blue line to Jean Talon (south exit). Walk west along Jean Talon to Henri Julien, then south on Henri Julien to the entrance.

ATWATER MARKET
138 Atwater
(514) 937-7754
Directions
Green line to Lionel Groulx. Walk south along Atwater to the market.

MAISONNEUVE MARKET
4445 Ontario St East (Letourneux)
(514) 937-7754
Directions
Green line to Pie IX (east exit). Walk south along Pie IX to Ontario, then east on Ontario to the market.

The Aquadome:
More Fun than Is Good for a Child

Bright and sunny, with floor-to-ceiling windows, LaSalle's community swimming complex, the Aquadome, is absolutely gorgeous. It just opened in 1996, so word is beginning to get around about its thoroughly modern facilities, pleasant staff and upbeat atmosphere. With an air temperature of 28°C and a water temperature of 30°C in the wading pool, it's a great place for kids. Whatever the season, whatever your age, drop by for a splash. The Aquadome is more fun than a barrel of wet monkeys.

The main swimming pool is 50 m long, but it is rarely open its full length. A moveable wall generally sits square in the middle, dividing the pool into a deep end (244–366 cm) and shallow end (maximum depth 152 cm). The deep end has two 1 m diving boards (open on weekends), and there are usually swimming lanes open in both ends for lap swimmers.

The star attraction is without a doubt the leisure pool, an extra-large multipurpose wading pool. One metre at its deepest, this amoeba-shaped pool is designed especially for youngsters, but there's something to rekindle the youthful spirit in just about everyone. A "beach" entrance beckons like an aquatic yellow-brick road. Designed as a gradual entry area for toddlers, it is 6 m wide and gently sloping, with tiling marking off the depth. The large mushroom-shaped fountain in the centre of the pool is always a hit. Water cascades off of it in great sheets. There is also a Jacuzzi area built into one corner of the pool. Cosy up for a therapeutic massage while keeping an eye on the kids.

But there's more. For the youngest children, there is a small blue slide in the beach entrance to be used under parental supervision. Next is the short but fun dual "pipe" slide leading into a deeper area of the pool. This one is for children under 122 cm who already know how to swim. For some real excitement, check out the two-storey-high combination of pipes and half-pipes. Complete with water jets to keep it slippery, this crowd-pleaser twists around in a complete figure-eight on its watery way to the wading pool. What a blast! To use this one you must know how to swim and be at least 122 cm tall.

Near the wading pool is an indoor patio area with room for a couple of dozen people, where you can pull up a chair to one of the tables or relax on a chaise longue. An outdoor terrace open in hot weather has room for 200 people, with many tables and umbrellas. You're welcome to bring your lunch to eat outside or to pick up something at the snack bar, located between the reception and the pool.

In addition to all the above, the Aquadome offers lessons in springboard diving, scuba diving, underwater hockey, life-guarding, instructing, first aid and health, plus a full range of physical fitness activities. Adults can swim to the soothing sounds of classical music on Tuesday nights, or New Age on Thursday nights.

The schedule at the Aquadome is rather complex and changes seasonally, as it is designed to accommodate three main groups: families, adults and seniors. The general hours and family hours are listed below.

1411 Lapierre St
(514) 367-6460

Season and Hours
General: 9 a.m.–4 p.m., except Tue 9 a.m.–1:25 p.m.
Family hours: Mon–Thur 5:30 p.m.– 7 p.m., Fri 5:30 p.m.– 9 p.m.
Leisure pool family hours: Mon, Wed, Thur, Fri 9 a.m.–3:55 p.m.
Big slide: Mon, Wed, Thur 1:30 p.m.–3:30 p.m., Fri 1:30 p.m.–3:30 p.m. and 6 p.m.–8:55 p.m., Sat–Sun 12 p.m.–7:55 p.m.
Diving boards: Sat–Sun 1 p.m.–4 p.m.
Musical swims (adults): Tue and Thur 9 p.m.–10:25 p.m.
Hours are longer in summer. Please call.

Fees
Adults $3, youth 4–16 $2, 3 and under $1, seniors $2. Reduced rates for LaSalle residents.

Directions
Green line to Angrignon. 113 or 113X bus to André Laurendeau College (corner of LaVerendrye and Lapierre).

Art with Clean Hands
at Paint-It-Yourself
Ceramic Cafés

BEACONSFIELD • DORVAL • NDG • DOWNTOWN

The first paint-it-yourself ceramic workshop appeared in New York city about five years ago. The phenomenon swept westwards and then returned east again. The café part is a Quebec innovation. Montreal now has four such cafés, two central and two on the West Island, where you can custom-decorate a plate, mug, vase—just about any household item you can imagine—without getting your hands dirty!

The basics are simple. Select an unpainted piece, pencil on a design and paint. Once you've finished, the pros take over, dipping the whole thing into a translucent glop—the glaze—and firing it at a scorching 982°C. In a few days, you return to collect the finished work. You pay for both the piece you paint ($4–$100) and for the studio time. The clock starts once you get your paints.

Here are some tips for first-timers:

- Be careful: Colours change dramatically with firing.
- Lack artistic skill? Choose an embossed design—it's like painting by numbers.
- Keep your hands clean. Even a little oil prevents the glaze from adhering.
- One coat for transparent coverage, three for opaque (coats dry in seconds).

Café Art Folie in NDG was the first of the now popular workshop-cafés in Quebec. The window is decorated with brightly painted wares, and there are comfortable couches by a small coffee and juice bar. The walls are lined with unpainted bears, business card holders, toothbrush stands, even a bust of Elvis. People work at half a dozen large tables. According to co-owner Tori Schofield, ceramic painting makes a great first date, since it "keeps your hands busy."

Café Art Folie has a **West Island** location, just opposite Fairview on St John's Blvd. This bright, cheerful place looks more like a trendy dessert bar than a workshop, and it does indeed serve scrumptious desserts. It also has a separate room for parties.

La Poterie in Beaconsfield is a cosy little café beside an art gallery. It has four large tables and walls lined with unpainted bisque, works in progress, and finished pieces on permanent display. This café appeals particularly to young families, as evidenced by the large Winnie the Pooh mural at one end and a reading table with books and Lego (for kids who get bored).

Co-owners Lisa and Holly see a lot of wedding showers and gift makers, plus others who come just for the health-minded fare (and sinfully delicious double chocolate-chip brownies) served in their restaurant. Like the other cafés, La Poterie has brushes and sponges to apply glaze, stencils to help with designs, and books and postcards for inspiration.

The newest, and biggest is the chic **Ceramic Café**. You could spend hours simply selecting a piece from among the thousands of Greek vases, gargoyles, medieval knights and more common household items on hand.

Professional artists can be found working here day and night, and several shelves of gallery-quality finished wares are on display for sale and inspiration. With an extensive menu and delicious desserts arranged on—what else?—brightly painted ceramic plates, this is also an interesting place for a snack, even if you're not going to paint. Smokers take cheer: this is the only ceramic café with a smoking section.

CAFÉ ART FOLIE
5511 Monkland Ave (Girouard)
(514) 487-6066

CAFÉ ART FOLIE
3339C Sources Blvd (Centennial Plaza)
(514) 685-1980

LA POTERIE
450B Beaconsfield Blvd (St Louis)
(514) 697-8187

CERAMIC CAFÉ
4201B St Denis (Rachel)
(514) 848-1119

For hours, fees and directions, see page 138.

Indoor
Karting

Grand Prix racing is a spectator sport that's all the rage with Montrealers. Hot on its heels is indoor karting, a scaled-down version that lacks none of the thrill of the real thing. It's fun, fast, friendly and exciting, but safety rules are taken seriously. If you've ever had a hankering to suit up, strap on a helmet, pull on some gloves and tear around a race track ... this is for you.

Most professional racers—our own Jacques Villeneuve included—got their start on large outdoor karting circuits, where speeds reach upwards of 100 km/h. Indoor karts weigh half as much and travel at about half the speed, but they are just as responsive and the track is that much tighter. When you're riding a few inches off the ground, negotiating sharp turns with another racer right behind you, the top speed of 60 km/h seems quite fast enough.

Whether you like it quick, slippery or technically challenging, you'll get a big kick out of the three indoor karting tracks in Montreal. Before venturing onto a course, first-timers get a polite lecture on the rules of the road: no bumping, obey the flags, keep both hands on the wheel and no fishtailing. You'll also get a few tips on handling hairpin turns: brake before the turn, enter it wide and accelerate out of it. Races last 10 minutes, and each car is equipped with a radio transponder that monitors lap time to a hundredth of a second. The clock starts after your first lap, so you can get to know the track. At the end of the race, you get a printout showing each lap time and your position in the race. (At most tracks groups can book the entire track for a "Grand Prix" evening with trial heats and final races.)

You'll feel like a pro at **F1 Indoor Karting,** where all drivers wear full racing gear, including a hairnet, gloves, a jumpsuit and a crash helmet. F1 was Montreal's first indoor karting track and by some standards it is the most technically difficult. You'll need to be handy with the gas and brakes to work the racing line on this 350 m concrete circuit that has plenty of curves, a lovely elongated S-curve and a double hairpin turn that will make your hair stand on end! The wide track has room to pass on its entire length. Marshals and assistants make sure everyone follows the rules—and get you going again if you spin out.

Circuit 500 offers the longest indoor track in the city, in a spacious warehouse. Three marshals are ready with flags to warn you if someone wants to pass, if there's trouble on the track ahead, or if you've broken a rule. The 700 m track is paved in asphalt so tires grip it like glue, paradoxically making it the fastest circuit on the island (since you can go faster without skidding.) It is a narrower track than the others, so passing is always a challenge, and the chicane will make you a master. The track area is lavishly decorated with flags and banners, and there is a large elevated observation deck.

Tires stacked three-high and held in place with a bright yellow rubber siding provide the visuals on the track at **Les Circuits In-Kart.** This newest arrival has a slick style inspired by European set-ups. Its wide 300 m concrete track was once covered with linoleum tiles, for a gleaming black surface that is somewhere between asphalt and concrete on the slippery scale. A prime shopping-mall location, tastefully decorated lounge and a conference room make this a popular spot for corporate get-togethers.

F1 INDOOR KARTING
1755 Fortin, Laval
(450) 629-2121

CIRCUIT 500
5592 Hochelaga
(514) 254-4244

LES CIRCUITS IN-KART
7852 Champlain, LaSalle
(514) 365-6665

For hours, fees and directions, see page 138.

Feeling Groovy
at the Émile Berliner
Sound Wave Museum
St Henri

When Edison invented the wax-cylinder phonograph in 1877, it changed the way people listened to music. Never before had there been a means to preserve sounds in an archive and replay them at leisure. In the hundred years since, a dizzying number of new technologies have been developed: LPs, 45s, two formats of CD, analogue and digital audiotapes. Music can now be delivered by radio wave, videotape, cable, Internet, and direct-to-home satellite.

At the Émile Berliner Sound Wave Museum in St Henri, the pace slows down. You can slip into the past for a leisurely look at the roots of recording and broadcasting, and at the man who spawned the modern music industry with an invention he called the record.

In 1877, 25-year-old Émile Berliner, a recent German immigrant, developed a carbon microphone that enabled Alexander Graham Bell to mass-market his recently demonstrated telephone. Berliner sold Bell the rights for $50,000 and used the money to fund further research in the budding field of communications. Ten years later, he made headlines with a recording and playback method superior to Edison's. It was a flat disc, engraved with sounds in a spiralling groove—not much different there. But it was more durable and, above all, much cheaper to produce than the competing cylinder.

The record, gramophone, and disc cutter Berliner invented were huge successes. You'd need a degree in business law to follow the mergers,

takeovers, licenses and lawsuits that created the modern record industry—
suffice to say Berliner was the father of it all. He founded the Gramophone
Co. of England (now EMI), the E. Berliner Gramophone Company of Montreal
(now part of RCA), and half a dozen other companies to produce records,
record players and radios.

The museum, in the building where he set up shop, is crammed with old
gramophones, wax-cylinder players and the first radio receivers and televi-
sions. A dedicated volunteer staff is busy repairing the donated equipment,
and many items are in perfect working order. Ask a guide to crank one up
for you.

Among other mysteries, the museum explains the origin of the little dog
listening to an old-fashioned record player that is still the trademark of RCA.
The dog's name is Nipper, he's a fox terrier and he was painted by British
artist Francis Barraud in 1899. The original painting had him listening to the
first Edison wax-cylinder type phonograph. Berliner bought the painting, but
not before he had Barraud paint over the Edison machine with one of his
own, the E. Berliner Model A Gram-o-Phone. A copy of the painting is on
display in the museum; the original hangs in EMI's head office in London.

The first records were made of zinc; a few years later of hard-baked vul-
canized rubber; and finally of a bizarre mixture of shellac, lampblack, cotton
flock and something called pyrites. In each case, the process was the same:
first a master disc copy was made on acetate using a disc cutter (one is on
display). Next it was chemically plated
with silver. Copper was applied to strength-
en the silver, in an electroplating process
that took 12 hours. The silver-copper surface was separated from the acetate to
form a new master.

To make the record, a hot mixture of
the latest compound was poured between
the masters, and the whole thing was
pressed under several tonnes of pressure.
Presto! One record, ready for hand-
polishing.

Now if someone could just explain CDs.

1050 Lacasse (de Richelieu)
Suite C-220
(514) 932-9663
Season and Hours
2 p.m.–5 p.m. Fri–Sun. Other days by
appointment for groups.
Fees
$3 per person.
Directions
Orange line to St Henri. Walk west on St
Jacques four blocks (against the traffic),
then north on Lacasse two blocks.

Rainy Day
Weekend Workshops
for Children

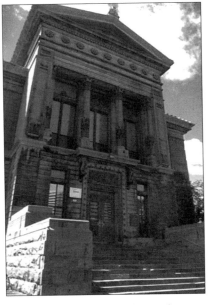

When the weather is lousy, entertaining children can be a chore. If you're going stir-crazy, Montreal's finest museums are there to help, offering inspired diversion for young ones and respite for parents most weekends of the year.

At the sleek, modern **Canadian Centre for Architecture**, workshops are organized in conjunction with exhibitions of interest to children, generally during the academic year, but sometimes in summer. They take place on both days of the weekend and are open to children ages 3–12. Children usually take a look at the temporary exhibition, then work on their own creations on an architectural theme. Reservations are required.

Every Sunday, year round, the **Montreal Museum of Fine Arts** hosts free workshops for children of all ages, on the 4th floor of the new building. Children visit the permanent exhibition, generally on a treasure hunt, before settling down to do a project. Around Christmas, for instance, youngsters hunted for angels in the artwork, then made angels themselves. Since the workshops operate on a first-come, first-served basis, it's best to show up early. Each session lasts about 45 min.

A little farther east is McGill University's **Redpath Museum,** a beautiful museum with a remarkable collection of Egyptian mummies, dinosaur fossils, rocks and mounted animals. Discovery Workshops are held almost every Sunday afternoon throughout the school year, one session for children ages 4–7 and another for those 8–12. There is a maximum of two children per adult, and you must register in advance by leaving your name, phone number and age of your child on an answering machine, Thursday mornings 9 a.m.–12 p.m. (The machine logs your time, so no early birds!)

The Museum of Contemporary Art (**Musée d'Art Contemporain**) is particularly convenient, since you don't have to leave the metro system to get there. Its Sunday-afternoon workshops put the emphasis on multimedia projects, using paint, collage and photographs, inspired by the modern works on display. (Despite the somewhat cerebral themes of the exhibitions, the workshops are definitely not stuffy: themes have included Charlie Brown, Whitney Houston and Pocahontas.) Workshops start on the hour, and you can stay as long as you like.

Finally, the **Marsil Museum of Costume, Textiles and Fibre** in St Lambert is a cosy little museum that's always kid-friendly. The Sunday-afternoon workshops, co-ordinated with each exhibition, are designed for children of all ages and are free with admission to the museum. Parents can stay with children during the workshop or visit the exhibition. Kids can stay as long as they like, and no reservations are required. (For a full write-up on the Marsil Museum, see page 136.)

CANADIAN CENTRE FOR ARCHITECTURE
1920 Baile
(514) 939-7026
Reservations required.

MONTREAL MUSEUM OF FINE ARTS
1379 Sherbrooke West
(514) 285-1600, ext. 135 or 136
First come, first served.

REDPATH MUSEUM
859 Sherbrooke West
(514) 398-4086, ext. 4092
Reservations required (phone Thur 9 a.m.–12 p.m.)

MUSÉE D'ART CONTEMPORAIN
185 Ste Catherine West
(514) 847-6253

MARSIL MUSEUM OF COSTUME, TEXTILES AND FIBRE
379 Riverside, St Lambert
(450) 923-6601

For hours, fees and directions, see page 139.

A Tourist
in Your Own Town with
Heritage Montreal

You can spot tourists a mile away. They are the ones actually stopping to look at things, often gazing above street level. What is it tourists see in a city that we seem to miss in our own? Find out on a walking tour with a volunteer organization dedicated to preserving Montreal's architectural treasures. Whether you take a walk designed for visitors or one of the neighbourhood walks especially for Montrealers, Heritage Montreal will help you see the city through fresh eyes.

Heritage Montreal has been offering walking tours of various historic neighbourhoods and parks for the past nine years, including the Lachine Canal, Mile End, St Henri, Westmount, NDG, downtown and Côte des Neiges, to name but a few. They also offer weekly tours of the Golden Square Mile and Dorchester Square. There are always two groups, one French and one English.

One sunny summer day, I went on a tour of one of my favourite areas: St Lawrence Blvd., a.k.a. the Main. The group met at the corner of Notre Dame and St Lawrence and walked slowly up to Bagg St (just north of Pine Ave). Our expert guide helped us make sense of the strip's eclectic jumble of buildings.

By the end of the 19th century, Montreal had a population of 250,000, making it the largest and most prosperous metropolis in Canada. Sherbrooke St, wide and modern, was considered the equivalent of New York's 5th Ave. But the mayor decided the city needed its own Champs Elysées as well, a wide boulevard that would be a mix of shopping, residential, industrial, commercial and cultural areas. Chosen for this grand task, the Main was widened by 6 m on its west side, between Notre Dame and Bagg.

A quarry on the corner of nearby Rachel and St Denis provided the greystone, and Chicago provided the style. After the Great Chicago Fire of 1871, architects used new techniques to quickly build edifices that were functional and elegant. With a structure of steel beams rather than wood, buildings did not need their exterior walls for support. This eliminated the "wedding cake" structure of older buildings and permitted taller structures with more windows. The façades were ornamented on the first two floors, had a plainer middle and were topped by a large decorative cornice.

Chinatown has some excellent examples of the Chicago style, at 974 and 1014 St Lawrence, in particular. Montreal's new buildings did not achieve the heights of Chicago's, but the architects took decoration to heart: the two-storey-high window bays of the middle floors of these two buildings are adorned with interesting checkerboard motifs.

Other highlights include the magnificent Monument National (at 1182). Built as a theatre, for many years it stood empty, but it now serves as the National Theatre School's principal venue. The large brick building occupying an entire block just north of Ontario was built as a tobacco company. It is currently owned by the Quebec Ministry of Cultural Affairs and is rented out as office space. On the northeast corner of Ontario and St Lawrence (2001) is the old Molson's Bank, Canada's first bank, now the Native Friendship Centre. Just up the street (2101-2111-2115), the Just for Laughs Museum, Cabaret Music Hall and LAM Importers occupy what was once a brewery.

The Parisian-looking building with dozens of curvy balconies on the southwest corner of St Lawrence and Sherbrooke is another marvel. It was built in 1910 using the then-new material of reinforced concrete. The architects were so pleased, they left the concrete exposed for all to see.

2180 Crescent
(514) 286-2662

Season and Hours
Architectours: Jun–Sept, Sat–Sun 2 p.m.
Golden Square Mile and Dorchester Square: Jun–Sept, Sat 10 a.m. Tours are rain or shine and last about 2 hr.

Fees
$8; members $6.

Directions
Golden Square Mile: Green line to McGill (McGill College exit). Meet on southwest corner of Sherbrooke and McGill College. Dorchester Square: Green line to Peel (Peel exit). Meet on southeast corner of la Gauchetière and Peel. Neighbourhood walks: Call for information on meeting places.

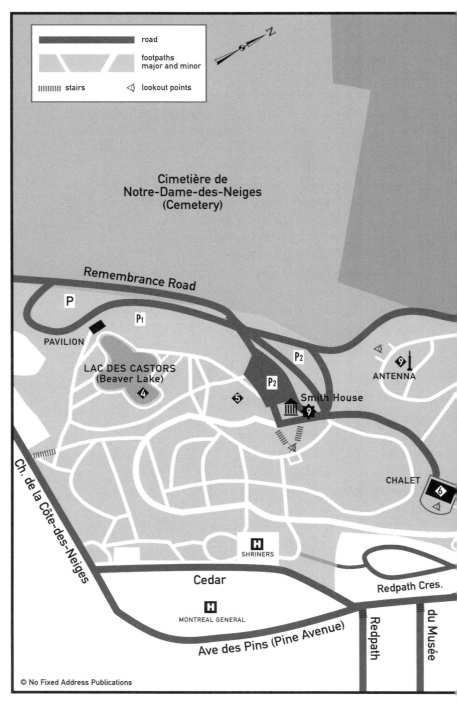

Cimetière de
Notre-Dame-des-Neiges
(Cemetery)

Remembrance Road

P

P1

PAVILION

LAC DES CASTORS
(Beaver Lake)

P2

P2

❹

❺

Smith House

ANTENNA

❾

❾

CHALET

❻

Ch. de la Côte-des-Neiges

SHRINERS

Cedar

Redpath Cres.

MONTREAL GENERAL

Ave des Pins (Pine Avenue)

Redpath

du Musée

road

footpaths
major and minor

stairs   lookout points

© No Fixed Address Publications

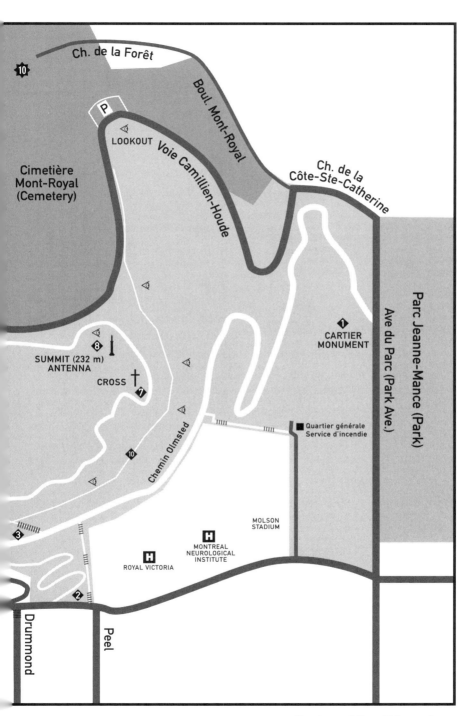

Ch. de la Forêt

10

Boul. Mont-Royal

P

LOOKOUT

Voie Camillien-Houde

Ch. de la
Côte-Ste-Catherine

Cimetière
Mont-Royal
(Cemetery)

CARTIER
MONUMENT

Parc Jeanne-Mance (Park)

Ave du Parc (Park Ave.)

SUMMIT (232 m)
ANTENNA

8

CROSS

7

Chemin Olmsted

10

Quartier générale
Service d'incendie

MOLSON
STADIUM

3

H
MONTREAL
NEUROLOGICAL
INSTITUTE

H
ROYAL VICTORIA

2

Drummond

Peel

The Essential
Mount Royal

No other landmark defines this city quite like Mount Royal. Since the park opened in 1872, Montrealers and visitors alike have been taking to the pathways, woods and slopes of the largest summit to stroll, cycle, relax and escape the urban environment.

Park designer Frederick Law Olmsted wanted visitors to leave the city behind and enter the relative wilds of the mountain gradually. His planned entrance at the Sir George-Étienne Cartier memorial facing Jeanne Mance Park (1 on map—see previous pages) is still popular. From there, a pedestrian road winds to the base of the escarpment and past Beaver Lake, ending at the chalet and lookout on the summit.

At the top of Peel St downtown, another path (2) soon joins Olmsted Rd. The well-maintained wooden stairway just east of the intersection (3) is a quick route to the top. For cars the Beaver Lake and Smith House parking lots (P1 and P2) are most convenient.

Beaver Lake (4) was added in 1937. Mount Royal may not be a mountain, but the lake is true to its name. Ancient beaver lodges were indeed found on the site, buried deep in the mud.

A statue garden (5) set in a glen is the result of a world symposium held here in 1964. While not to everyone's taste, the pieces represent significant works of artists from nine countries. A leaflet for a self-guided tour is available from Smith House (see pages 30–31).

The chalet at the summit lookout (6) was built in 1903 of stones quarried on the mountain. Fossilized worms and coral—500 million years old— are visible in the walls. The chalet has a pretty good snack bar, film and souvenirs, and peanuts for the squirrels. The lookout offers a great view of downtown. A by-law forbidding construction of buildings taller than the mountain has been respected, though one preserving sight lines to the river is largely ignored.

From the chalet you can take a meandering loop around the summit past the famous cross. The original cross (location unknown) was planted by city founder de Maisonneuve in 1643. The modern structure (7) was erected in 1924. Recently new lights were installed that can be changed to purple at the flip of a switch, to mark the passing of the Pope. The big white needle farther along (8) carries communication signals. The huge red and white broadcasting tower (9), known as the CBC tower, actually transmits nine radio and four television stations.

There are two fine viewpoints on this upper loop. Both look out over Camillien Houde Rd, with views of St Joseph's Oratory and the Université de Montréal's distinctive tower. Houde, mayor of Montreal and one of the park's greatest defenders, was quoted as saying there'd be a road through it over his dead body. He wasn't wrong. The road was built when he died, and named after him to boot.

While rich for an urban park, the trees are rather sparse all over the mountain. In the early '50s, Mayor Drapeau had many of the larger trees cut down in an attempt to curb licentious behaviour. All the pine trees you see are the result of replanting.

For the most striking views, take the less visited Escarpment Trail (10). Created in '94, this marvellous walk provides unusual perspectives over east central downtown and the Plateau district. To find it, head to the left of the chalet lookout (facing the city). The trail starts at the top of the wooden staircase.

General info (Tues-Fri): (514) 872-6559. Lookout chalet (snack bar): (514) 872-2033. Beaver Lake chalet (snack bar): (514) 872-2969. Les Calèches André Boisvert (carriages): (450) 653-0751.

Season and Hours
Park: Closed midnight–sunrise. Beaver Lake chalet: 8:30 a.m.–9:30 p.m. Lookout chalet: 8:30 a.m.–8 p.m. Snack bar hours vary, generally 10 a.m.– 4 p.m.

Fees
Park: Free. Parking: $1.25 per hr, max $3.75 per day ($1, $2, 25¢ coins). Horse and carriage (24 hr notice required): 30 min $30, 1 hr $50.

Directions
Jeanne Mance entrance: Green line to Place des Arts and 80 bus north to Rachel (half-way up Jeanne Mance Park). Beaver Lake and Smith House: Orange line to Mont Royal and 11 bus west. Or, Green line to Guy and 165 bus to Remembrance Rd, transfer to 11 bus east. Peel entrance: Green line to Sherbrooke and 144 bus west along Pine. Or, Green line to Peel and walk north on Peel.

9

Mount Royal's Surprising
Smith House

Mid-19th century Montreal was not a happy city. It was in the midst of an economic depression brought on by a change in international trade laws, a huge fire had wiped out 1,100 homes in one day, and the city was plagued by epidemics of cholera and typhoid brought from Europe by impoverished Irish immigrants.

At the time people thought diseases were spread by miasmas, poisonous vapours arising from swamps, and cities were generally unhealthy places to live. Sunshine and fresh mountain air were one of the few preventions and cures in the days before antibiotics. In 1858 merchant and farmer Hosea B. Smith bought two large bands of land on Mount Royal. Away from the city—without even a view of it—he built a solid stone farmhouse and moved his family to the cleaner climes of the mountain.

The sturdy rough greystone house still stands and is now home to a fine, informative museum run as the Centre de la Montagne. The three-room museum departs somewhat from the new trend of interactive displays without much text. There are magnifying glasses and insects for kids to view, but there's plenty of reading for adults, especially city residents who want to learn a little bit about the social, environmental and even economic history of the mountain.

While not the site of the fabled Iroquois town of Hochelaga, the mountain did have a large Native presence. Several Indian graveyards have been discovered, as well as a rock quarry for tool making. On display are arrowheads, cutting tools and some of the most sophisticated Iroquoian pottery ever found.

Under European settlement, the mountain was privately owned by some of the wealthiest families in Montreal, including the Redpaths (of Redpath Sugar) and the Allans (the country's richest family at the time). As early as the 1850s, there was talk of turning the mountain into a municipal park. But when the Lamothe family clear-cut their land—there's a photo of the resulting mess in the museum—the city was spurred into action. Nine lots were expropriated and the park was created in 1872. The total price: just under a million dollars—a bargain, even in today's dollars ($80 million).

Well-known American park designer Frederick Law Olmsted (architect of Central Park, Capitol Hill Park and many others) was called upon to lay out the park. He didn't think much of it as a mountain, declaring that if it weren't in the middle of the city we wouldn't even call it a hill. But he saw its value as a park, and even broke with his own habits by designing paths that followed the natural contours of the landscape.

The museum reveals some surprising facts. For example, hidden away beneath various peaks and hills are reservoirs containing all the city's drinking water. Under the main peak is one the size of seven olympic swimming pools. (You can tell which reservoir serves your district by the colour of your fire hydrants.) It also explains the origin of the city's name. When Jacques Cartier climbed the mountain in 1535, he christened it Mont Royal (for King Francis I). But Cartier's cartographer was an Italian, Giovanni Battista Ramusio, so the first maps bore the name Monte Real, which became, in time, Montreal.

The Centre de la Montagne hosts a number of events on the mountain. In May, birdwatching walks and the annual mountain cleanup are held. Every Sunday in October full-day hikes take you to all three summits—Westmount, Murray Hill and Mount Royal—plus the cemeteries. Smith House is also home to Les Amis de la Montagne (Friends of the Mountain), a lobby group.

1260 Remembrance Rd
(514) 843-8240

Season and Hours
10 p.m.–5 p.m. Closed Christmas and New Year's Day.

Fees
Museum: Free. Parking $1.25 per hr, max $3.75 per day ($1, $2, 25¢ coins).

Directions
Orange line to Mont Royal and 11 bus west. Or, Green line to Guy and 165 bus to Remembrance Rd, then transfer to 11 bus east.

The Hidden Treasure of
the Mount Royal
Cemetery

As anyone who has visited Mount Royal park can tell you, a great deal of the mountain appears to be taken up by an enormous graveyard. What might not be immediately obvious is that there are actually two: the Catholic Notre Dame des Neiges and the multidenominational Mount Royal. But the real surprise might be that the Mount Royal Cemetery is arguably the prettiest part of the entire mountain, if not the island. It is a giant garden of flowering shrubs and bushes, rare trees and songbirds set in 67 ha of rolling hills and valleys, very much concealed from the rush of the city.

Designed in 1852 by American J. C. Sydney as a garden cemetery—there are only three such cemeteries on the continent—it flows with the natural terraces and contours of the mountain. As you stroll its many roads and footpaths, one section at a time is revealed, giving the illusion of greater size and space while remaining intimate and serene. The smell of wild thyme underfoot mixes with lilacs, crab apple, peonies or roses, depending on the season.

Three pamphlets available the from office have terrific maps and excellent write-ups to help you locate points of interest, whether birds, plants or historic graves. You can also call ahead to arrange for a free guided tour in English or French.

The cemetery boasts dozens of varieties of flowering and fruit-bearing shrubs and trees, and numbers over 10,000 carefully tended trees of over

500 varieties. The plantings are mostly the work of the superintendents, all of whom traditionally have strong horticultural backgrounds.

To the left of the office, on a large lawn beyond a little brook, is the city's oldest gingko tree. The fan-shaped leaves of this 20 m Japanese tree make it hard to miss. There is also a very interesting tree, called a metasequoia, near the Lilac Knoll. Planted in honour of botanist Ernest Henry Wilson, this deciduous-coniferous tree has the needles of a juniper bush, but unlike most conifers, it loses them in winter. The cold climate has stunted its growth—it should be dozens of metres high, but it looks like a bush. Wilson travelled the world collecting new species of plants for Harvard University. He died in a car accident while visiting Montreal.

If you're looking for historic graves or simply remarkable ones, you'll find them everywhere. The oldest graves are in section A2. Among the fading sandstone tombstones, a small metal cross marks the tomb of Chief Joseph Onaskenrat (1845–81), the first Indian buried in the cemetery. The chief from Kanesetake (just off the West Island) converted his tribe to Methodism after land-use disputes with the Catholic church. According to his death certificate, he died of "congestion of internal organs." Some suspect he was poisoned.

The firemen's graveyard (section G1) features a huge pedestal topped by a fireman, with small markers for those who died on duty. One of the saddest areas is the children's cemetery (section G3). Many of the miniature tombstones have a sorrowful little lamb sitting on top.

Fans of pop culture will want to seek out the graves of the six *Titanic* victims buried in the cemetery. There is a Molson (section F1), and four members of the Hays family (Pine Hillside). Whatever you are looking for, the helpful staff at the office can indicate sites on a map.

1297 De la Forêt (Forest Rd)
(514) 279-7358
Guided tours with advance reservations. Maps available from gatehouse on left-hand side when office is closed.

Season and Hours
Office: Mon–Fri 8 a.m.–5 p.m., Sat 9 a.m.–3 p.m., Sun phone calls only. Main gate (Forest Rd): Every day during daylight hours. South gate (Remembrance Rd): Closed to vehicles from 4 p.m. Sat–Sun.

Fees
Free.

Directions
Office and main gate: Green line to Édouard Montpetit. Walk east on Mount Royal to Forest. Remembrance Rd entrance: Orange line to Mount Royal. 11 bus up mountain to south gate (where road begins to descend again).

Letting off Steam
at the
Colonial Baths

Between 1880 and 1920, Montreal saw a large influx of eastern European immigrants, who brought with them the grand old tradition of the "*shvitz*," or steam bath. When Aaron Adler built the Colonial Baths in 1914, access to the Turkish (wet steam), Russian (dry steam) and Finnish (dry) saunas would cost you a quarter. You'll pay more than that now, but the Colonial Baths—still owned by the Adler family—are still a bargain. And while many bath houses have a reputation for being gay gathering places, at the Colonial Baths the clientele is generally a fifty-fifty mix of gay and straight, and everyone seems to get along fine.

When you enter the bathhouse you are handed a bar of soap, a couple of towels, a sheet and a key. A central locker room has a couple of rows of divans to relax on. Just off the main area is a TV room where you can snack (one group of older men feast there weekly, and outside meals are welcome). Another room has a few pieces of exercise equipment.

The shower area and saunas are through a glass door and down a short narrow flight of stairs. This is a world of heat, humidity and tiles. The showers, the stairs, the walls—everything but the ceiling—is tiled in white and spotlessly clean.

SPA

Film buffs will recognize the Russian sauna from *The Apprenticeship of Duddy Kravitz*. Its layout, mode of operation and scorching temperatures haven't changed in 80 years. Three-tiered wooden benches have room for a dozen or so, while a large oven set into the wall provides the heat.

To up the heat in the sauna, you swing open the heavy oven door and toss a bucket or two of water onto the enormous rocks. Be sure to stand aside. Inside the oven, the temperature is a singeing 180–200°C. The water instantly comes rushing back out in the form of invisible steam.

The Turkish steam bath is unique in Montreal. Most steam rooms pump out clouds of steam automatically, at regular intervals. Here you control it using a large valve. The steam issues from behind and beneath the wooden benches. If you bring your own essential oil, a few drops against the wall behind the benches will turn the steam bath into a whole new experience. A self-administered cold bucket of water over the head also does wonders.

The whirlpool bath is rather tame, but pleasant nevertheless. A large button on the wall turns on the jets, and elegant marble dividers make getting in and out easier. Another way to relax is in the cedar-panelled Finnish sauna, a small room that seats about six.

For an unforgettable experience, allow master masseur Garry to take you on "a trip to a steam bath in Siberia." His world-famous cedar-broom soap massage begins with cold towels on your head and feet. He dunks a thick branch with dried leaves into a bucket of soap suds. As he briskly rubs you up and down, the rich, earthy smell of the leaves transports you to distant forests. Next he expertly removes the last few decades of dead skin with a giant loofah, in a process that remains just this side of flaying.

If you feel you can never be too relaxed, continue the pampering with a marvellous oil and alcohol massage. Garry combines massage and acupressure techniques to undo the knots of daily life, rubbing you down with plain or scented oil. If he detects a misaligned bone or two, Garry, who studied medicine in Russia, will set things right. All this to the soothing tones of Russian opera.

3963 Coloniale
(514) 285-0132

Season and Hours
Every day from 1 p.m.. Women's day is Tuesday.

Fees
Adults $13; admission and roomette $15; soap massage, steam room or shower $8 (10–15 min); steam room and shower $14; hot oil massage $12 (20 min).

Directions
Orange line to Sherbrooke (St Denis exit). Walk north on St Denis to Pine, then west on Pine to Coloniale, and north on Coloniale.

A Romantic Lunchtime Cruise on the *Île de France* ... at Eaton's

The 1920s were the heyday of the great ocean liners. Between the wars, and before the market crash and Great Depression, the cruise-ship business flourished. Liners with names like *Leviathan, Olympic* and *Aquitania* crisscrossed the Atlantic, taking the wealthy on holiday cruises to foreign ports. A 30-day cruise to the Middle East cost $400, and a shot of whiskey set you back 15 cents. Those days are gone, but a moment of this deluxe splendour has been preserved in Montreal—not in dry dock or a dusty old museum, but in Eaton's department store, in the heart of the city.

The French Line's *Île de France* was a latecomer to the scene. She was launched in the spring of 1927, at a time when the great liners were already a vanishing breed. She was one of the grandest passenger vessels ever, half the size of the ill-fated *Titanic* (1912), but twice as luxurious. Each of her over 400 first-class cabins was decorated in a different art deco design, a new and controversial style at the time. She also had the longest bar in the world, measuring 10 m. With Prohibition in Canada and the States, it was undoubtedly a popular gathering spot.

In her 12 years of service, the *Île* ferried a quarter of a million passengers between the two continents, including such well-known names as Maurice Chevalier, J. D. Rockfeller, Tallulah Bankhead and Sam Goldwyn. Anyone who was anyone took a cruise on what was known as "the flapper of the flappers."

At some point the passenger list included Lady Eaton (daughter-in-law of store founder Timothy.) So inspiring did she find the ocean liner's magnificent art deco dining room that she challenged French architect Jacques

Carlu to reproduce it on the 9th floor of the downtown Eaton's store, as the chain's flagship restaurant. The 9ième opened on Monday, January 26, 1931, and hasn't changed a bit since.

Stepping into the restaurant, you are transported to another world. The dining room is enormous and opulent, yet understated, with seating for 500 at bistro-style tables. Its perfect symmetry highlights the strong lines, stainless steel and pastel colours that are hallmarks of art deco.

Directly opposite the entrance is the original stainless-steel buffet, built at a cost of $30,000. Ten metres above is the nave, decorated with softly lit bas-relief plaster badges depicting game, fruit and other gastronomic delights. Over the nave are long horizontal frosted windows, admitting natural and artificial light. All this is supported by a dozen tall pink and grey marble columns.

At either end of the restaurant are Pre-Raphaelite murals featuring nymphs and does, painted by the architect's wife, Natacha Carlu, and clearly inspired by the artwork on the ship. Beneath the murals are fountains trickling into a basin. Steps leading to this level are flanked by large alabaster vases illuminated from within, on black marble pedestals.

The restaurant went through a dark period in the '70s when the crisp white linen cloths were replaced with a red checkerboard pattern, but all is well again. The tables are laid with Royal Doulton china and silverware. The à la carte menu, rich and varied, remains affordable, though most people prefer the hot and cold buffet with dozens of main courses, a cornucopia of seafood, salads, and the expertly carved traditional roast beef *au jus*. There is also a pasta table, specials of the day, six kinds of wine by the glass, and dozens more by the bottle. The service is excellent.

For an enchanting afternoon, why not take your sweetheart on a luncheon cruise in the heart of Montreal? The 9ième is a gem. All that's missing is the world's longest bar and a couple of staterooms!

677 Ste Catherine West
(514) 284-8421
Reservations recommended for groups of 6 or more.

Season and Hours
Mon–Sat 11:30 a.m.–3 p.m., Thur 11:30 a.m.–3 p.m. and 4:30 p.m.–8 p.m., Sun 10:30 a.m.–3 p.m.

Fees
Buffet $12.50, children $6.25; table d'hôte $8.75; à la carte prices vary. Wine and taxes not included.

Directions
Green line to McGill. Enter Eaton's. Elevator to 9th floor.

Showing You the Money at the Stock Exchange

If you think high finance is all dreary men in pinstripe suits, drop in on the first stock exchange in the country. The seemingly free-for-all action on the trading floor is anything but dull—even the thick glass of the visitor's gallery isn't enough to block out the shouts of the traders. To help you make sense of it all, there is a very slick visitor's centre and an excellent guided tour.

You'll learn all the basics on the one-hour tour: what stocks are, what makes share prices go up and down, and the different kinds of securities traded on the world's markets. You'll also learn to read a ticker, and by extension the newspaper listings. The Montreal Exchange even has its own Web site for Internet surfers who catch the trading bug.

Half a dozen stations provide a basic introduction to the stock market, from its earliest form—purchasing the right to buy olives in ancient Greece—to its most modern. Many are interactive. At one particularly good station, you select three imaginary stocks from various industries. Next you watch a news broadcast relating world events and local business news and try to predict the effect on your stocks: Will the prices go up, go down or remain unaffected? Once you've made your guess, the simulator takes over and you can watch the prices change. Afterwards, an explanation is given for the results.

One end of the visitor's centre overlooks the trading floor, a large paper-strewn room crowded with people, computers and LED displays. To the left is the stock-trading area. The door on the left in the back leads to the stock-options area. Bond futures are to the right.

The most exciting area is where traders bid to purchase government bonds at specific interest rates, on specific dates in the future—bond futures. It is a traditional "open outcry" floor, where bids are yelled out just like at a public auction. While open outcry floors are fast disappearing—Paris and Sydney just closed theirs—the Montreal Exchange maintains that it results in faster, more efficient trading.

In any event, it is a great lesson in how the market works. Members of the exchange sitting on the sidelines receive orders from their brokerages by telephone. They signal their pit men, who use a combination of hand signals and shouting to make deals with their counterparts from other brokerages. When a deal is struck, they write it down on a pit card. Runners (often pit men in training) take the cards and enter the data into amber-screen terminals off to the side. At the same time, six exchange operators watch the action from a raised platform in the centre and record the trades in their own computers, for display on the big board's ticker. All this takes place in a matter of seconds.

In addition to brokerages, there are 100 individual members trading in bond futures. To become an individual trader, you must buy a seat on the stock exchange ($6,000), take a special course ($2,000) and maintain a minimum account balance ($25,000). Of course, you must also have nerves of steel.

For members of the general public who want to learn more about the market or improve their trading skills, the stock exchange offers two levels of introductory courses and a number of advanced courses at very reasonable prices.

800 Victoria Square
(514) 871-3582
Reservations required for groups of 15 or more.

Season and Hours
Visitor's centre: Mon–Fri 8:30 a.m.–4:30 p.m. Tours: May–Sept 10 a.m. (French) and 1 p.m. (English).

Fees
Free.

Directions
Orange line to Victoria Square. Escalator and stairs (or elevator) to lobby, then elevator to 4th floor.

Two Special
Skating Rinks

Though only about two-thirds the size of a hockey rink, the **Bell Amphitheatre** is without a doubt the city's nicest indoor skating rink. Light streams through the huge atrium over the rink, and a cheerful attitude prevails. The temperature is a comfortable 20°C on the ice and 23°C in the food court gallery that overlooks it. Understandably, most people skate without hats or gloves. Lockers are available.

The quality of the ice is also a boon. It is resurfaced every hour or two by a special electric Zamboni (most are propane powered). In addition, demineralized water is used, for denser ice less prone to chipping.

In case you've ever wondered, here's what goes on inside a Zamboni: A horizontal blade scrapes the surface, while a jet of water cleans the ice and is quickly vacuumed up. From the back end of the machine, hot water is poured onto the ice in a fine layer. The water not only runs into any cracks or skate marks, it melts the existing ice to refreeze in a surface that's as good as new.

Saturday mornings from 9–11 are reserved for adults with children under 12, and Friday nights you can skate to the tunes of a live DJ (requests are taken). You can also celebrate birthdays on the rink, with helmets, lockers and a cake for $5 per child.

If you're an outdoor skater who likes an early start or late finish to the season, the Old Port's **Bonsecours Basin** is the place to go. Located on an island in the artificial basin between the Jacques Cartier and Clock Tower piers, this rink affords a spectacular view of Old Montreal and the modern skyline beyond. It is the only refrigerated outdoor rink in the city, for excellent skating in the shoulder seasons and during those rare mild spells in winter.

The rink is cooled by close to 30 km of 2.5 cm diameter pipes running through its concrete base. Units with the combined power of 750 home refrigerators maintain the 4.5 cm of ice at the optimal temperature of −8°C, and a Zamboni keeps the ice in tip-top shape. An additional skating area of natural ice on the basin itself is opened when the ice is safe.

It may be cold outside, but the Bonsecours Pavilion is always warm, with changing rooms, a central area and a small snack bar. Skate rental and sharpening services are available.

Skating is free on the Bonsecours Basin, but parking is pricey in the port-side parking lot and difficult to find in the streets. Watch out for metered residents-only parking zones! It is an easy, if sometimes windy, walk from the metro to the river.

Note: At neither the Bell Amphitheatre nor the Bonsecours Basin are you allowed to skate with infants in your arms or shoulder packs. Toboggans can be rented for towing children around the ice. Deposits and ID are required for skate rentals. Helmets are required at the Amphitheatre for children under 6.

BELL AMPHITHEATRE
1000 de la Gauchetière West
(514) 395-0555
Season and Hours
11:30 a.m.–10 p.m. daily, till midnight on Sat.
Fees
Adults $5, under 16 $3. Disco night (16+) $5. Skate rental $4, helmet rental $1.50. Sharpening $4.
Directions
Orange line to Bonaventure. Follow signs.

BONSECOURS BASIN
Old Port (514) 496-PORT (7678), Bonsecours Basin (514) 283-5256
Season and Hours
10 a.m.–10 p.m. daily, early Dec – early Mar. Closes 6 p.m. Christmas and New Year's.
Fees
Skating free. Skate rental $6. Sharpening $5. Lockers free ($2 for lock). Parking $7.
Directions
Orange line to Champ de Mars. Follow signs to Vieux Port, or walk south on Gosford St.

Halloween
in the City

Halloween is a special time of year in Montreal. Our four scientific centres—the Planetarium, Botanical Garden, Insectarium and Biodome—add to the fun by banding together to celebrate all things spooky. For a skyward look at Halloween, visit the **Planetarium**, where a special show explains the mysterious tradition of dressing up and getting candy. According to the presentation, Halloween is an ancient Celtic harvest festival marking the start of winter (Nov 1 by the Celtic calendar)—and the transition from autumn to winter, lightness to darkness, and life to death.

On Oct 31, spirits rose from the grave to descend into darkness. The Celts extinguished the fires in their fireplaces to make their homes look abandoned and left food on their doorsteps to placate the spirits. If they went out, they would dress up as spirits themselves to fool the real ones. Aha! Now it all makes sense.

The show also tours Montreal's night sky, pointing out the (fictional) Vampire and Cat constellations. It also relates several eerie stories sure to raise gooseflesh on younger audiences.

At the **Botanical Garden**, one end of the main greenhouse is decorated with hundreds of pumpkins. But these are no ordinary *Cucurbita pepo*; these pumpkins are imaginatively decorated with paint, beadwork, papier maché and carving. It's all part of an annual contest, with entries from all over the province in several categories. Over the years, pumpkins have cropped up as fruit (apples, watermelons, tomatoes), animals (cows, dogs, porcupines) and various objects (vacuum cleaners, jars of jam). More ambitious themes (globes, farmland, horse-drawn carriage) have also been tackled. One or two prize-winning giants have weighed in at over 250 kg.

What would Halloween be without a gander at a swarm of giant Madagascar cockroaches? You'll find these 7 cm beauties (and other creepy-crawlies) at the **Insectarium**, safely behind glass. At Halloween, children can have their faces painted with spider designs, take a peek at live tarantulas and other spiders, and learn a little about these often maligned creatures in the "Spiders Unmasked" presentations, every half hour on weekends (French only). For example, did you know spiders have no ears or noses? I guess that rules out eyeglasses!

The **Biodome** is the newest science centre. It contains four compact but remarkably effective ecosystems. At Halloween, the spotlight is on bats. There are 460 of them living in a cave, where day and night have been reversed, making them active during visiting hours. Halloween brings with it bat theatre, bat workshops and the chance to touch a live bat.

PLANETARIUM

1000 St Jacques West (Mansfield)
(514) 872-4530

Season and Hours
Tues–Sun 1:15 p.m., 8:30 p.m.;
Sat 1:15 p.m., 3:45 p.m., 8:30 p.m.
(French); 3:30 p.m., 7:15 p.m. (English).
Halloween shows: Oct 10–Nov 2.

Fees Adults $6, students and seniors $4.50, youth 6–17 $3.

Directions Orange line to Bonaventure. Walk south on Mansfield or de la Cathédrale. Turn west on St Jacques.

BOTANICAL GARDEN AND INSECTARIUM

4101 Sherbrooke St East (Pie IX)
(514) 872-1400

Season and Hours
Gardens, greenhouses, Insectarium:
9 a.m.–5 p.m. Halloween shows:
9 a.m.–9 p.m., early Oct –early Nov.

Fees Adults $9.50, youth 6–17 $4.75, seniors $7.

Directions
Green line to Pie IX. Walk north on Pie IX (or 139 bus north one stop) to Sherbrooke, then walk east to entrance.

BIODOME

4777 Pierre de Coubertin
(514) 868-3000

Season and Hours
9 a.m.–7 p.m.

Fees Adults $9.50, students and seniors $7, youth 6-17 $4.75.

Directions
Green line to Viau. Follow signs.

Getting Hooked ... on
Indoor Climbing
Gyms

Y ou don't have to be muscle-bound to do well at rock climbing. More than strength, climbing requires agility, flexibility and grace, at least in the early stages. While the sport was originally practised by men, nowadays women make up almost half its enthusiasts. Indoor climbing is a thrilling sport that invigorates as it relaxes, where the first hurdle you encounter is the one you've imposed upon yourself.

Most newcomers begin with an introductory course. You'll learn how to put on the harness, tie a special knot and act as belayer. Climbers always work in teams: while one climbs, the belayer attends to the safety rope attached to the climber, looped over a bar at the top of the wall and back down. The belayer takes up the slack as the partner climbs and rappels the climber back to the ground. A friction brake means that even those unmatched in weight can be a team.

On the wall, handholds vary from large and nubby to just barely visible. Climbing "routes" are laid out by experts, and the degree of difficulty is indicated at the bottom of the wall. Hand-holds are often colour coded, allowing several routes in the same climbing area. For an easy route, for example, you might use only the green handholds. Routes are changed regularly.

Allez-Up has the style and ambience of a modern art gallery. This very mellow and welcoming environment has all the ingredients for good indoor

---

climbing—dozens of routes at varying degrees of difficulty, overhangs, cornices, traverses and roofs. It also has the highest walls in the country, towering 14 m above a very Zen pea-gravel floor. Large windows admit plenty of sunshine, and rhythmic music sets the tone for what is always a good climb.

LaSalle's **André Laurendeau College** had one of the first climbing walls in Montreal. It began serving its own students during the day and the general public in the evening six years ago. One room contains challenging 10 m walls, while a second has an extensive overhang for ridge traverses, a grotto for that cave experience and Montreal's most spectacular roofs, for dozens of metres of completely inverted climbing.

At the University of Montreal's huge athletic complex, **CEPSUM**, there's always activity in the climbing area, where you can get a bird's eye view of the tennis courts, running track and indoor golfing sandtrap—but you're better off keeping your eyes on the wall! Uncrowded climbing, with tips from the experts on most Tuesdays and Thursdays.

Action Directe in Laval is the newest climbing gym, having opened its doors in December. The warehouse, with funky light green, orange and yellow walls, popular roof areas and a grotto with roof-top exits, attracts some great young climbers. Action Directe also has Montreal's only outdoor climbing wall.

Finally, **Horizon Roc** is a marvellous set-up just east of the Olympic Stadium. Natural light and 12,000 square feet of climbable walls make this the largest climbing gym in the country and a great place to get started. There's plenty of space for lead-climbing, a large grotto for going upside-down and a bouldering area providing plenty of challenges for advanced climbers. This place also has the largest play area especially designed for children.

ALLEZ-UP
1339 Shearer (SE corner at St Patrick)
(514) 989-9656

ANDRÉ LAURENDEAU COLLEGE
1111 Lapierre (La Verendrye)
(514) 364-3320, ext. 249

UNIVERSITY OF MONTREAL CEPSUM
2100 Édouard Montpetit (SW corner at Vincent d'Indy)
(514) 343-6150, (514) 343-6993

ACTION DIRECTE
4377 St Elzéar West (Curé Labelle)
(450) 688-0515

CENTRE D'ESCALADE HORIZON ROC
2350 Dickson (SW corner at Hochelaga)
(514) 899-5000

For hours, fees and directions, see page 139.

17

All Aboard for the
Train Exhibitions!

Autumn is model-train season, with two big exhibitions open to the public. Both events have a festive atmosphere and some really amazing train set-ups. They are also great places to meet experts or pick up missing items to get your own set running again.

The **Montreal Railroad Modelers' Association** holds its open house in late October. Its clubhouse, located directly under the entry ramp at Central Station, is a train lover's dream. The periodic rumbling of trains passing overhead provides a realistic soundscape for the miniature world within its walls.

The biggest train layout in the country takes up most of the main room. (A smaller room houses an N-scale set that is almost as impressive.) About 25 HO-scale locomotives run through a wonderful world that includes a fishing village, hydro dam, steel mill, prairie scene, huge city, and bridges and towns too numerous to count. The mountain that dominates one end of the track took three years to build, and the brewery is an exact replica of Molson's London plant. In all, the layout measures 39 m by 12 m and trains take several hours to go all the way around.

A high-tech system is needed to control the 480 switches as up to a dozen trains circulate simultaneously on track that, laid end-to-end, would stretch for 2 km. At the hub, 4 human operators wearing headsets issue orders to up to 12 others in the various yards—the main yard is 13 tracks wide. A closed-circuit television helps yardmasters keep an eye on the far side of Crystal Spring Mountain, and LEDs on a control panel light up to indicate the trains' positions.

Club members take the game seriously. Waybills are issued for goods to be delivered. A dispatcher tells drivers where to go and how long it should take them to reach each destination. Each detail of a large operation is carefully enacted, even to the point of "changing crews" in the city. Part of the pleasure, according to members, is simply seeing your own train travelling through so much beautiful scenery.

Things are in full swing during the annual open house, when half a dozen other clubs move in for the weekend to display train sets of all shapes and sizes. One man has two large suitcases (and a very small train) called Valise East and Valise West. Other clubs inter-connect their sets, and dozens of merchants and collectors are on hand, selling new and used trains and accessories.

At about the same time of year, train aficionado Ivan Dow presents the **Montreal Model Train Exhibition**, a fund-raising event for **Sun Youth** featuring dozens of layouts, merchant stalls and hands-on fun in the best show in town for kids.

This exhibition brings together model railroaders from all over Quebec, Ontario and the United States. Layouts range in size from the 4-in-wide tracks of the G-scale monster (designed for outdoor gardens) to the diminutive Z-scale trains, small enough to travel through a tunnel in a large peanut. The Canadian Railway Museum, Wakefield Steam Engine and other important organizations also participate.

There's always a play area where children ages two and up can monkey around with different kinds of trains, and some years a car race-track is set up for older children. Mr Dow's own Thomas the Tank Engine layout is always a big hit. It puffs steam and goes "peep, pip, peep" just like the real thing.

MONTREAL RAILROAD MODELERS' ASSOCIATION
891 St Paul West
(514) 861-6185
Season and Hours
Sat 11–5 p.m. and Sun 10 a.m.–4 p.m., weekend closest to Nov. 1. Call to confirm exact weekend.
Fees
Adults $5, children under 12 $2, families $10.
Directions
Orange line to Bonaventure (St Antoine exit). Walk south on University, then west on St Paul to the red door under the tracks.

MONTREAL MODEL TRAIN EXHIBITION
350 St Paul East
(450) 659-9745, (514) 872-7330
Season and Hours
Sat–Sun 10 a.m.–5 p.m., early November. Call to confirm exact weekend.
Fees
Adults $5, seniors $4, children $2.
Directions
Orange line to Champ de Mars (Vieux Montreal exit). Walk south on Gosford (up the hill) then east along Notre Dame. Turn south on St Claude and continue to Bonsecours Market.

The Rise and Fall
of a Working Class
Neighbourhood

Most museums honour the achievements or display the possessions of the rich, powerful or famous, but this one is swimming upstream. The Écomusée du Fier Monde—the Proud World Ecomuseum—honours the working people that fuelled Canada's industrial revolution from the mid-'18th century until the late '50s. Occupying a restored public bathhouse dating from the '20s, it is a modern, well-designed museum that feels like installation art.

The pool has been drained, and the tiled floors replaced with bright hardwood, but the atmosphere has been faithfully preserved. The original marble staircase leads from the attractive entrance to the mezzanine. From there you enter directly into the large art deco bathing area, with high arched ceilings and expansive glass-brick windows. The permanent exhibition is mounted in "beaches"—alcoves surrounding the pool on two levels. The basin of the old pool houses the temporary exhibitions.

The museum documents the rise and fall of the neighbourhood in a dozen thematic niches outlining living and working conditions from 1850 to the present. The small settlement that began in 1769 when Molson's set up a brewery boomed when the industrial revolution came to Canada in 1850. Over the next hundred years, the district saw incredible growth as it dominated the Canadian textile, food and manufacturing scene. Now called Hochelaga-Maisonneuve, it was affectionately known as the "Faubourg à M'lasse" (Molasses Town) for the molasses reservoirs that loomed large on the landscape until the 1950s.

The displays don't mince words about the stark realities of the lives of the workers. Pushed from the countryside by larger farms and advancements in machinery, the workers lived seven or eight families to a triplex, with court-yard lodges taking the overflow.

With 8–10 children per family, conditions were crowded, to say the least. In fact, a public inquiry in 1899 found that children as young as seven were working 12 hours a day, 6 days a week. It also found that the city had the second-worst infant mortality rate in the world, just behind Calcutta.

In the next two decades things began to improve with the introduction of neighbourhood health clinics, pasteurized milk and the building of the public bathhouses. A total of 16 opened in the '20s and '30s for labourers and factory workers, whose crowded homes didn't have showers or baths. The baths provided private stalls for showering and a swimming pool for recreation—some even had bathtubs. Three days a week were for men only, two days for women; on weekends children were allowed. The museum's Généreux Baths were the busiest, receiving 87,000 visitors in 1940 alone.

In less than a generation, globalization and deindustrialization of the first world hit the neighbourhood hard. From 1950 to 1970, factory after factory shut. In what must surely rank as one of the city's most short-sighted solutions, it began expropriating the workers' houses and tearing them down: 100 were torn down to build the Université du Québec à Montréal; 250 for the construction of Dorchester Blvd (now René Lévesque); 678 to make room for the CBC tower and parking lots.

Despite the presence of these new institutions and a more recent infusion of cash by restaurateurs and club owners in the Gay Village, the district remains relatively poor. The population is about a fifth what it was in '50s, unemployment ranks at 20%, and 30% of the residents are single parents. Nevertheless, a community that was once bound together by work, religion and necessity now finds strength in over 100 grass-roots organizations, at the centre of which is the Écomusée du Fier Monde.

Displays are written up in French only.

2050 Amherst (Ontario)
(514) 528-8444
Season and Hours
Thurs–Sun 10:30 a.m.–5 p.m.,
Wed 11 a.m.–8 p.m.
Fees
Adults $4, seniors and students $3, children 7–12 $2, families $10.
Directions
Orange or Green line to Berri-UQAM. Walk east along de Maisonneuve or Ontario to Amherst, then north on Amherst. Or, Orange line to Sherbrooke. Walk south on Berri to Sherbrooke, then east on Sherbrooke to Amherst and south on Amherst.

Getting
Off the Island
Without a Car!

Winter, spring, summer or fall, it's hard to beat a day out on the trails. But if you don't have a car, getting there can be a challenge. Take heart! Whether you're single and looking or settled with kids, in great shape or in the mood for a nice stroll, there's a hiking club for you. While the focus in this discussion is on warm-weather activities, the groups offer winter outings, too. And the best part is that transportation is arranged.

If you're not sure how far you can hike, try a "tourist walk" with **Randonnées Plein Air** (Outdoor Walks). On these trips along country roads and quiet lanes, the bus follows at a distance, catching up on occasion for those who want a rest. Slightly more challenging "health hikes" take place in parks in town and out. If you're in good shape, try a European-style "Audax" walk, a 25–100 km hike at a brisk 6 km/h. This mainly French-speaking club also offers mountain walks and hikes, and long-weekend getaways to destinations such as Amish country in Pennsylvania. Most excursions include a cultural activity at the end of the day. Trips are by bus.

The newest club, **Nature Trek** (a.k.a. Joie du Plein Air), puts the emphasis on the simple enjoyment of nature. Founded in 1995, this lively club attracts an equal mix of English and French, ages 25–55. Groups are limited to 15 people. There are always two outings each weekend: one easy and one more difficult, ranging from forest strolls on nearby Mount St Bruno to the ups and downs of New York's Sawteeth Mountain. The increasingly popular "exploratory hikes" are mushroom-picking expeditions, frog-calling walks, trips to bat caves and the like, led by expert naturalists. Nature Trek keeps costs down with car-pooling.

For over 30 years, **JASS**, Montreal's premier singles' club, has been hitting the road at a leisurely 9:30 a.m.–11:30 a.m., depending on the destination. Best known for its weekend walks on Mount Royal and Mount St Bruno—happy hour follows the Mount Royal hike—the club also offers more adventurous day-long excursions onto Quebec's country trails. Here again, the emphasis is on socializing, since you gather for a group lunch at the top of the mountain. JASS also offers Friday night dances, classical music evenings and a host of other activities. Car pools leave from the Crémazie and Longueuil metro stations.

Dozens more hiking clubs are affiliated with the **Fédération Québécoise de la Marche** (514-252-3157). Each season the federation publishes *Marche*, a great magazine that includes a list of clubs and calendar of events.

RANDONNÉES PLEIN AIR
(514) 524-5925. Reservations required.
Season and Hours All year.
Fees Hikes $40–$45 (includes bus fare).
Directions Bus leaves from north exit of Crémazie metro station (Orange line) at 7:30 a.m.

NATURE TREK
(JOIE DU PLEIN AIR)
(514) 721-3375. Reservations required.
Season and Hours All year.
Fees Hikes $21 non-members, $14 members; car pooling $7–$10/day; membership $39.50/year.
Directions Car pools leave from Henri Bourassa (Orange line) (trips north) and Georges Vanier (Orange line) (trips south and east) at 7–9 a.m., depending on destination.

JASS
(514) 388-8727. Reservations required.
Season and Hours All year.
Fees Mount Royal & Mount St Bruno: non-members $6; members $3; car pooling $1/30 min; membership $40/year.
Directions Mount Royal: Sat & Sun 2 p.m. SW corner of Park and Mount Royal. Mount St Bruno: Car pools leave from Mount St Bruno shopping centre. Other destinations: Car pools leave from Crémazie (Orange line) or Longueuil (Yellow line) metro stations at 9:30–11:30 a.m., depending on destination.

Old Montreal

⊙ Cobblestone streets and bustling squares ... Tall, narrow buildings echoing with the clatter of horse-drawn carriages ... Modern fun in old-fashioned surroundings is what attracts residents and visitors alike to Old Montreal. You could spend hours simply wandering around, inline skating on the waterfront promenade, or browsing in the galleries and boutiques along St Paul

Street. ⊙ Interested in history? Old Montreal is the place to go. Its museums specialize in telling the story of this old port town, and are the finest, most approachable museums in the city. Have kids in tow? Wow them at the IMAX theatre, get them lost in SOS Labyrinthe, even take them on an inexpensive

ferryboat ride across the St Lawrence. And you can't miss Place Jacques Cartier. Bordered by restaurants, the city's oldest and liveliest square is the hub of activity in the area.

✪ Note: Parking is very difficult in Old Montreal, and residents-only zones often have parking meters, which can be confusing. As in other areas of the city, the ticketers are ruthless. Public parking on the Quai de l'Horloge (the Clock Tower Pier) and the Alexandria Pier is safer, but much more expensive. Your best bet is to take the metro.

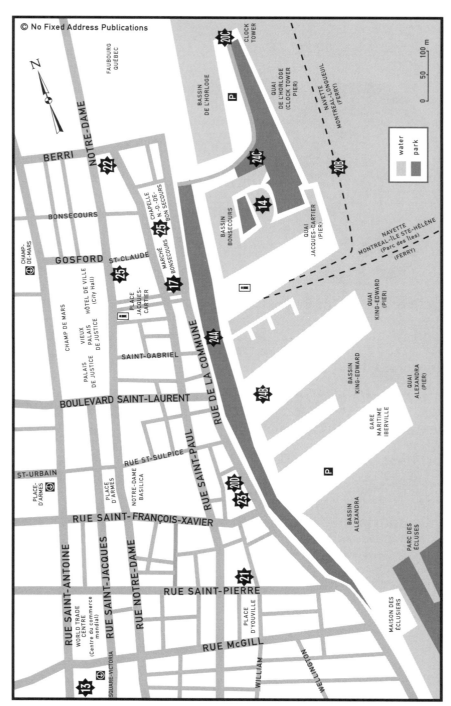

© No Fixed Address Publications

TRIP DESTINATIONS
(denoted by star symbol on map)

20A. Notre Dame de Bon Secours Chapel
450 Saint Paul East
(514) 282-8670
p. 56

20B. Croisières AML (ferries)
Jacques Cartier Pier (foot of St Lawrence)
(514) 281-8000
p. 56

20C. Clock Tower
Quai de l'horloge (Clock Tower Pier)
(foot of Place Jacques Cartier)
(514) 496-PORT (7678)
p. 56

21. Centre d'Histoire de Montréal
335 Place d'Youville
(514) 872-3207
p. 58

22. Sir George-Étienne Cartier Museum
458 Notre Dame East
(514) 283-2282
p. 60

23. & 20D. Pointe à Callière Museum of History and Archaeology
350 Place Royale
(514) 872-9150
p. 62 & p. 56

24A. Promenade
(514) 496-PORT (7678)
p. 64

24B. IMAX
King Edward Pier
(514) 496-IMAX (4629)
p. 64

24C. MayaVentura (maze)
Quai de l'horloge
(Clock Tower Pier)
(514) 869-9919
p. 64

25. Château Ramezay
280 Notre Dame East
(514) 861-3708
p. 66

13. Stock Exchange
800 Victoria Square
(514) 871-3582
p. 38

14. Bonsecours Basin
(514) 496-PORT (7678)
p. 40

17. Montreal Model Train Exhibition (Bonsecours Market)
350 St Paul East
(514) 872-7730, (450) 659-9745
p. 46

TOURIST INFORMATION

Old Port of Montreal Tourism
Jacques Cartier Pier
(514) 496-PORT (7678)

InfoTourism Old Montreal
174 Note Dame East
(Place Jacques Cartier)

20

The Best Views
in Old Montreal

When Montreal's first chapel was built in 1675, it was just outside Ville Marie and 30 m from the shoreline. The city has changed names, and the river has been pushed back. But **Notre Dame de Bon Secours**, rebuilt once due to fire, is still magnificent, and for a view over the rooftops, there is no finer address to call in on.

An enclosed wood balcony overlooking the waterfront leads to the tower and gives a foretaste of the sights to come. It is an easy climb to an enclosed viewpoint decorated with stained glass—but watch your head on the spiral staircase! A few more steps take you to the outdoor belvedere, level with two trumpet-bearing angels and directly under the 6 m statue of the Virgin Mary, arms raised in blessing. What a welcome sight the steeple must have been after a long and perilous sea voyage to a strange new land.

An excellent museum in the chapel pays homage to Marguerite Bourgeoys. This intrepid woman worked tirelessly to establish the chapel and first school, crossing the Atlantic seven times to better the life of the colonists. Fifty-eight delightful dioramas and three high-tech holographic movies present scenes from her life. A crypt, discovered during renovations in 1998, contains the foundations of the original stone chapel. Artifacts unearthed are presented in showcases.

Looking rather lonely on the tip of the bent arm of a long pier, the **clock tower** is one of the Old Port's most attractive structures. It was commissioned to honour missing wartime sailors, but the realities of life in a working port soon forced alterations upon Paul Leclaire's 1919 design. From a 30.5 m abstract pink granite monument it evolved into a concrete and stucco clock tower sturdy enough to support grain conveyors. Now standing solo, the tall structure marking the eastern limit of the Old Port has nevertheless retained a light and airy look.

There are 135 steps up to the works and another 56 to the lookout. Panels and photos explaining the history of the port lure you ever upwards and provide ample excuses to rest. Some explain the economic evolution of the port, while others intrigue with messages such as "plans to fire a cannon at noon were abandoned." Soon you are at the base of the 6.1 m pendulum; next you are practically inside the works of the clock, right behind the four huge faces.

From the top the views along all four points of the compass are excellent. To the north is the city centre, due east is the Jacques Cartier Bridge, west is the Victoria Bridge—the city's first—and to the south is the lighthouse on St Helen's Island.

Croisières AML operates a number of the ferries in the Old Port. The cheapest way to get out on the water is to take a trip to St Helen's Island or Longueuil. The route to Longueuil is best, taking you past the new port and under the fabulous Jacques Cartier Bridge. It also connects with a cycling path that shadows a busy highway and leads to the Boucherville Islands, a rather urban park. The ferry to St Helen's Island is free if you visit the Biosphere or the Stewart Museum at the Fort. No charge for bicycles.

For the best view while dining, head to the terrace of **Pointe à Callière** (see page 64).

NOTRE DAME DE BON SECOURS CHAPEL
450 St Paul East
(514) 282-8670

CLOCK TOWER
Quai de l'horloge (Clock Tower Pier)
(foot of Place Jacques Cartier)
(514) 496-PORT (7678)

CROISIÈRES AML (FERRIES)
Jacques Cartier Pier
(foot of St Lawrence)
(514) 281-8000

For hours, fees and directions, see page 140.

21

Montreal at a Glance in the
Centre d'Histoire
de Montréal

It is hard to imagine a better place to get to know the city than this sandstone and brick fire station in the Old Port. The museum is a living,
breathing map of the city past and present. Within the space of an hour
or so, you can get a remarkable feel for the city by strolling its neighbourhoods, visiting its factories and docks—even visiting a typical dwelling—all
in the comfort of a thoroughly modern museum.

The museum is a masterpiece of *trompe l'oeil* design. Each of its seven
main rooms is packed with things to look at and listen to. Displays re-create
different periods of Montreal's history and interesting neighbourhoods using
perspective and lighting to powerful effect. Some displays light up as you
approach; others remaining dark until you press a button.

In one room you'll find yourself beside the Romanesque pillars of the
Bank of Montreal building; just a few feet away are the neo-Gothic arches of
Notre Dame Basilica. You'll walk across a wooden pier in the Old Port under
the bow of a large wooden sailing ship, then "ride" a rambling streetcar along
Ste Catherine Street. The different areas are gracefully connected by corri-

dors, arched doorways, ramps and staircases (though the museum is fully wheelchair accessible).

This is a history lesson that even children will enjoy. There is only one item that isn't to be touched: a lamppost of raw fibreglass, from Expo '67, on display in the lobby. Everything else is hands on, including a turn-of-the-century oak timeclock (made by IBM!) that gives a very satisfying, resounding clang when you press a lever. Most displays have plenty of push buttons, and exhibits are designed to be viewed for around two minutes apiece.

One of the most remarkable areas is the exhibit of the traditional working-class neighbourhood of the Plateau Mont Royal. It features an excellent model showing a backyard view of a typical triplex. It also has an almost full-scale re-creation of the façade of a duplex. If you don't live on the Plateau, this is your chance to climb one of its famous curving wrought-iron and wood staircases. Unique to Montreal, these veritable works of art were often designed on the fly for each particular home. Leading from the sidewalk to the second-floor balcony, they saved space (and eliminated the need to heat a stairwell) by moving the entire affair outside.

Up top, you enter into the small living room of a well-kept home, with a comfy chair and a 1920s-style radio "broadcasting" a lively show. A little farther on, you can peek into an alleyway through the knotholes of a tall fence.

Another spectacular display presents Montreal in the mid-1800s, when it led the way in the Canadian industrial revolution. Subdued lighting, life-sized photographs of workers, and gigantic belts and pulleys spinning in slow motion overhead give an otherworldly feel to what must have been, in reality, an overwhelmingly noisy environment.

Note: While the multimedia displays are bilingual, written information is in French only. However, at the reception desk you can pick up a booklet that has the translated text of each display.

335 Place d'Youville
(514) 872-3207

Season and Hours
9 a.m.–5 p.m. daily, May 4–June 21; 10 a.m.–5 p.m. daily, June 22–Labour Day; 10 a.m.–5 p.m. Tues–Sun, Labour Day–May 3. Closed second Monday in Dec to Dec 31.

Fees
Adults $4.50; youth 6–17, students and seniors $3. Reduced rates with Access Montreal card.

Directions
Orange line to Victoria Square (St Jacques exit). Walk south on McGill College, then east on Place d'Youville to the museum.

22

Mysterious Traditions Revealed at the Sir George-Étienne Cartier Museum

Modern-day Montrealers have a good deal in common with the Victorian middle class of a 100 years ago. The homes of wealthier city dwellers of the late 19th century were cluttered with travel souvenirs: Greek busts, Japanese vases and so on. The Great Exhibition of 1851, housed in London's Crystal Palace, had presented goods from all over the world. Displaying a similar sense of worldliness was important to the Victorians.

A slice of Victorian life in turn-of-the-century Montreal is preserved at the Sir George-Étienne Cartier National Historic Site, a cosy museum located in the eastern end of Old Montreal on the corner of Notre Dame and Berri streets. The museum is in two lovely old adjoining buildings formerly owned by Sir George-Étienne Cartier: Montreal politician, lawyer and Father of Confederation.

You enter through the carriageway into the more modern half of the house, then wander through six or seven rooms, including a sitting room, Mme Cartier's bedroom and a lavishly decorated dining room. Don't forget to peek into the bathroom, for a look at a rare commodity in those days: a bathtub. Its dull hue has nothing to do with age or lack of scrubbing. It was produced in the days before ceramic glazing, when the first tubs were made of lead.

The museum explains a few mysterious traditions that have stuck with us, such as armchairs for men and armless chairs for women, still commonly seen in dining rooms. This seemingly strange pattern dates back to the time when women's huge dresses required special seating. The panel in front of the sitting-room fireplace was also a Victorian invention—to protect the "delicate skin" of the fair sex from the heat.

Interestingly, in French homes, the husband and wife sat opposite one another at the centre of the dining table. In English households, they sat at the ends. George-Étienne was an anglophile, and his wife, Hortense (Fabre), a francophile. Despite their many Victorian trappings, at mealtime, they sat at the centre.

Perhaps the most interesting tradition we owe to the Victorians is that of the Christmas tree. In 1873 a Christmas photo of Queen Victoria published in the *Illustrated London News* showed her and her family beside a small table-top pine tree, decorated with paper ornaments, with gifts underneath. This was a tradition in Germany, where Victoria's mother and husband were from. Christmas as a children's celebration was new to the English-speaking world, but soon everyone was following the lead of the tree *and* the gifts.

At **Christmas** the museum really comes to life, as staff deck the halls, banisters and tables, and generally put on a really good show. On weekends bilingual "servants" dressed in their Sunday stand by to explain the Christmas customs of the Victorian bourgeoisie. For example, on special occasions arrangements of fresh fruit sat on the sideboards, though not the table. But not all was to be eaten—the pineapple, a novelty, was too costly. It was rented for the occasion and had to be returned! The Victorians also brought canned food to the table—in the cans, which were an exciting new invention.

Guided tours (English and French) take place regularly during the Christmas schedule, and are available for groups at other times of year, with advance notice.

458 Notre Dame East
(514) 283-2282
Groups requiring tours must reserve.

Season and Hours
Apr 1–June 24 and Sept–Dec 20:
Wed–Sun 10 a.m.–12 p.m. and
1 p.m.–5 p.m.; June 24–Sept:
10 a.m.–6 p.m. daily. Closed
Dec 21–Mar 31.

Fees
Adults $3.25, seniors $2.50, children
6–16 $1.50.

Directions
Orange line to Champ de Mars (Vieux
Montreal exit). Walk south on Gosford
(up the hill) to Notre Dame, then east to
museum.

23

18th-Century
Market at Pointe à Callière

In the early summer of 1642, Paul Chomedey Sieur de Maisonneuve stepped ashore on a muddy point of land jutting out into the St Lawrence, establishing the first European settlement, a religious colony, on the island of Montreal. The colonists had a difficult time of it. Almost half their number died that first winter, and a good many more would have if not for the kindness of the Native people. With the first warmth of spring came the annual flooding of the river, driving the missionaries to higher ground. (The cross on Mount Royal is in memory of the settlers, replacing the one erected by de Maisonneuve as a promise to God if he spared further lives.)

On the 350th anniversary of Montreal's founding, the Museum of History and Archaeology opened on the very spot of the first settlement. It is an odd-looking building, designed by Dan Hanganu to reflect Montreal's historic and nautical past. Its triangular shape is a nod to the Royal Insurance Co. building that once stood there and is evocative of a ship's prow. The high tower and exposed "ribbing" are also reminiscent of a ship, and the exposed gallery has a monastic feel to it.

To take you into Montreal's past, the museum leads you beneath the cobblestone streets of the Old Port. During excavation for the museum's foundation, important structures and artifacts were unearthed. The remains of the St Pierre River now runs through the basement. Like most of the island's streams, it was enclosed in a culvert, this one in 1849. There is a little water in it most of the year, more in springtime. A surprising discovery was the first Catholic cemetery, its graves long forgotten beneath the foundations of an 18th-century warehouse. Like the other finds, this, too, was incorporated into the museum.

It is fascinating to walk through the subterranean excavations, among massive fieldstone foundations that include the Wurtele Inn and an old guardhouse, and right over a model of Montreal as a walled city in the mid-17th century. You'll also get the chance to meet ghostly innkeeper Sarah Wurtele, who can answer questions about Montreal.

Every August the museum hosts a very popular open-air market. It took two years to put together the list of about 35 Quebec artisans who make goods that would have been found in the markets of the mid-18th century: lace, baskets, straw hats, beeswax candles, shoes, chocolate, goat's-milk soap and more. All merchants don period costume and many demonstrate how they make their wares. One year a man sheared sheep using foot-powered clippers, and a woman washed clothes in the fountain of Place Royale.

There is food and drink, too, including blueberries from Lake St Jean and mead. Some current staples are notable by their absence. Tomatoes were formerly believed to be poisonous, and potatoes were considered animal fodder—so you won't find any fries and ketchup. What did teenagers eat? Well, chewing gum, any-way—one man sells a very spicy pine-resin chewing gum made from an old recipe. The flavour lasts for weeks.

At **Christmas** the museum brings together Santas from around the world. Some years you'll meet Italy's Befana, Spain's Melchior or Russia's Babushka; and you can always count on our own Santa Claus and St Nicholas to be there. All Santas are bilingual and can tell the story behind their gift-giving traditions.

350 Place Royale
(514) 872-9150

Season and Hours
Museum: Labour Day–June 24: 10 a.m.–5 p.m. Tues–Fri, 11 a.m.–5 p.m. Sat–Sun; June 24–Labour Day: 10 a.m.–6 p.m. Tues–Fri, 11 a.m.–6 p.m. Sat–Sun. Market: 10 a.m.–8 p.m. Sat, 10 a.m.–6 p.m. Sun, usually last week-end in Aug.

Fees
Museum: Adults $8.50, seniors $6, students (with ID) $5.50, children 6–12 $3, family $17. Outdoor market: Free.

Directions
Orange line to Place d'Armes. Go south on St Urbain (becomes St Sulpice) to de la Commune. Head west to museum.

24

Keeping Kids Happy
In Old Montreal

After the face painting, street performers and ice-cream stands of Place Jacques Cartier, much of the kid-friendly activity is to be found across the tracks and inside the confines of the Old Port. For the city's 350th anniversary in 1992, the warehouses, piers and 2 km promenade were spruced up considerably, and each year new businesses open. You'll pay for entertainment south of de la Commune, but that's how it goes where tourists congregate. Here's a run-through of the main children's attractions.

Now under a big-top tent on the Clock Tower Pier, **MayaVentura** is a high-tech maze designed to confuse and confound. Special bracelets register your success as you make your way to four Mayan "temples" in a maze that can be played at five levels of difficulty. Guides on inline skates roam the corridors to help you find your way ... and lose it again. Watch out—If a sign says "shortcut," it probably isn't one! On special summer evenings, the lights are turned out after 8 p.m., and you must find your way by flashlight (bring your own or purchase on site). The tarpaulin-hung frames that create the corridors are rearranged weekly. The maze is wheelchair and stroller accessible.

JUNE/DEC

Most people are familiar with the giant-screen thrills IMAX has to offer. The IMAX theatre at the Old Port was Montreal's first and it still boasts the largest screen in town. Its double features regularly include 3D films. The program changes twice a year, in April and September.

For a bit of free fun, make your way to the Jacques Cartier Pier, where kite-maker Claude Thibaudeau has his gang demonstrating the art of **kite flying**. Every weekend of the year, about a dozen or so single stringers and the more controllable double-lined kites take to the air, weather permitting. You can try your hand at flying, too—but first you've got to drop by his boutique at 224 Saint Paul St West to get a flight pass. It's free, and the Cerf-Volanterie is worth a visit just to see the amazing variety of hand-made kites there. Prices start at $65.

Two- and four-seat four-wheeled cycles can be rented from **Quadricycle** for use on the promenade. Half an hour is ample for a leisurely pedal up and down. To pedal about on the water, rent a **pedalboat** on Bonsecours Basin. Don't worry about drifting into shipping lines; this artificial basin is completely enclosed.

Velo Aventures has enough stock to put 250 people on wheels—inline skates, bicycles, tandems, baby joggers and children's trailers. (If you've never learned to ride a bicycle, owner Ken Piché will teach you, with guaranteed results.) You can also rent inline skates at two stores on de la Commune St.

Keeping adults happy is not a problem either. One of the biggest events at the Old Port is the annual **Beer Mundial**. Each year in late June, brewmasters from around the world come to present their wares, and the festival now boasts 250 varieties of beer and scotch, with local breweries solidly represented. Prices are too high to really indulge, but it's a good opportunity to sample.

At **Christmas**, an outdoor stage is built and bleachers are set up for a living nativity scene. Actors sing and live animals—including sheep, goats and a camel—contribute to a convivial atmosphere, whatever the weather.

Vieux Port de Montréal
(514) 496-PORT (7678)
MayaVentura
(514) 869-9919
IMAX
(514) 496-IMAX (4629)
Quadricycles
(514) 849-9953
Pedalboats
(514) 282-0586
Velo Aventure
(514) 847-0666
La Cerf-Volanterie
(514) 845-7613

For hours, fees and directions, see page 141.

The Château Ramezay Museum—
the Who's Who
of Old Montreal

Place Jacques Cartier is Old Montreal's liveliest square. But for the movers and shakers of yesteryear, look to the stone manor house nestled on its edge, facing city hall. The Château Ramezay Museum houses odds and ends ranging from a penny-farthing bicycle to a prayer book in Micmac and the "missing" church bell from Louisbourg. It also features fabulous portraits and early landscapes. It's a who's who of Old Montreal, New France and Quebec, telling the story of the French, English, Scots and Irish that settled and built the city.

The solid stone structure was built in 1705 as the Ramezay family dwelling. The name sounds Scottish, but it's actually French. Saved from the wrecking ball by a group of concerned citizens in 1896, the building has been lovingly preserved ever since. Indeed, it would have been a difficult building to knock down. Some exposed floorboards measure 12 x 12 inches (30 x 30 cm), and were fitted to be air- and watertight, since the chateau was later used as a storehouse as well as an office.

The exhibits in the many small rooms of the museum are arranged chronologically and thematically. The first presents precolonial Indian life on the island and features a superb scale model of an Iroquois village. Highly interesting is the colourful self-portrait by the last chief of the Hurons. Beside it are many of the items he is seen wearing, including an ornate combination peace pipe and war axe. There is also a portrait of Jacques Cartier, the first European to reach Montreal (1534). But it is an artist's invention: No one knows what the explorer actually looked like.

One of the most impressive rooms reproduces the wood-panelled head office of La compagnie des Indes, France's crown corporation for trade in the East Indies, which occupied the building from 1756. The richly worked walls were brought from the company's head office in Nantes, France, for display in the French pavillion at Expo '67 and acquired by the museum shortly thereafter.

One room is devoted to the Patriot Rebellion of 1837, in which French and English common people led by Papineau and McKenzie rebelled against the elitist provincial government. In it hangs a picture of Lord Elgin with the declaration he penned assuring all victims of the Rebellion would be reimbursed for their losses. This declaration enraged the English, who torched the houses of parliament, in Montreal at the time. The portrait was Elgin's favourite, donated by his descendants.

Another fine portrait is of Jean Talon, New France's most progressive Intendant. Under Talon, captains and soldiers—not just nobility—received lands. He also brought the *filles du Roy* (literally the King's daughters) over to marry colonists. Talon was big on marrying. Eighteen-year-old women and twenty-year-old men not yet hitched were slapped with fines. Single men also lost their rights to hunt.

It may seem strange to see Benjamin Franklin's portrait in the museum. But he came to Montreal when American troops invaded and occupied the city for several months, using the chateau as their headquarters. They unsuccessfully attempted to convince Quebeckers—under British rule at the time—to join their fight against the British. Franklin left behind his printing press and printer. In 1778 Fleury Mesplet started the Montreal *Gazette*. He was repeatedly thrown into jail for expressing his views on liberty.

On Sunday afternoons families can learn to bake bread or make butter in the antique kitchen. Regularly scheduled Sunday concerts are well attended. In July '99 the museum will unveil the outdoor Governor's Gardens.

280 Notre Dame East
(514) 861-3708
Season and Hours
10 a.m.–4:30 p.m. Tues–Sun;
Summer: 10 a.m.–6 p.m. daily.
Fees
Adults $6, seniors $5, students $4,
youth 6–18 $3, family $12.
Directions
Orange line to Champ de Mars. Walk,
following signs to Vieux Montreal/
Old Montreal.

West Island

⚙ The West Island begins in historic Lachine and stretches 20 km to the Lake of Two Mountains, where the Ottawa River meets the St Lawrence. Many people equate the West

Island with suburban homes and strip malls, but in fact some of Montreal's finest nature escapes are found here. ⚙ Cap St Jacques Nature Park, for example, is a gem. A third larger than the park on Mount Royal, its has deep woods, great walking trails and a busy beach. The vast area was once entirely rural, and there are still two working farms: McGill's Macdonald Farm and the Eco-Farm at Cap St Jacques. There's history, too, in the charming Lachine Fur Trade Museum. ⚙ This section also presents a few destinations not technically on the West Island, but well worth going the extra mile. Pointe du Moulin, on nearby Île Perrot, has one of the oldest operational windmills in Quebec. It's also a great place for a stroll or picnic. Oka Park, well known for its tremendously popular beach, has two excellent fall hikes and trails for skiing, too. ✿ Not all the destinations in this section are easy to get to by public transportation. The Ecomuseum and Morgan Arboretum are only accessible in rush hour during the school year. Pointe du Moulin requires a long taxi ride. In these and other cases, driving directions are given.

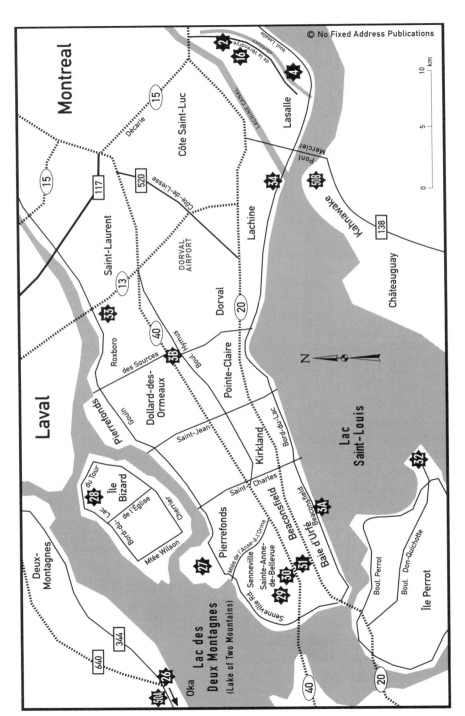

TRIP DESTINATIONS
(denoted by star symbol on map)

26. Oka Park
2020 Chemin d'Oka
Oka
(450) 479-8365
p. 72

27. Cap St Jacques Nature Park
20099 Gouin Blvd West
Pierrefonds
(514) 280-6871
p. 74

28. Bois de l'Île Bizard Nature Park
2115 Chemin Bord du Lac
Île Bizard
(514) 280-8517
p. 76

29. Morgan Arboretum
150 Chemin des Pins
Ste Anne de Bellevue
(514) 398-7812
p. 78

30. Ecomuseum
21125 Chemin Ste Marie
Ste Anne de Bellevue
(514) 457-9449
p. 80

31. Macdonald Farm
21111 Lakeshore Rd
Ste Anne de Bellevue
(514) 398-7701
p. 82

32. Pointe du Moulin
2500 boul Don Quichotte
Notre Dame de l'Île Perrot
(514) 453-5936
p. 84

33. Bois de Liesse Nature Park
9432 Gouin Blvd West
Pierrefonds
(514) 280-6729
p. 86

34. The Fur Trade Museum in Lachine
1255 St Joseph
Lachine
(514) 637-7433
p. 88

2. Aquadome
1411 Lapierre
LaSalle
(514) 367-6460
p. 14

3A. La Poterie Ceramic Café
450B Beaconsfield Blvd (St Louis)
Beaconsfield
(514) 697-8187
p. 16

3B. Café Art Folie
3339C Sources Blvd (Centennial Plaza)
Pointe Claire
(514) 685-1980
p. 16

4. Les Circuits In-Kart
7852 Champlain
LaSalle
(514) 365-6665
p. 18

16. André Laurendeau College (rock climbing)
1111 Lapierre
LaSalle
(514) 364-3320, ext. 249
p. 44

TOURIST INFORMATION

MUC Nature Parks Info Line
(514) 280-PARC (7272)

Laval-Île Bizard ferry
(450) 627-2526

26

A Marsh Walk and Religious Pilgrimage in
Oka Park

Oka Park is well known for its beach, but this enormous park has a rich variety of terrain and two terrific walking trails. One is an easy stroll, the other is uphill in the footsteps of tens of thousands of pilgrims. Popular all year, both these hikes are excellent in the autumn.

The **Grande Baie** trail starts at the visitor's centre just inside the park and leads to a spectacular marshland on an enormous sheltered bay. The pea-gravel and packed-earth trails are generally in very good shape, with a few uneven patches. It is a mainly easy walk, though there are one or two steeper hills.

The first part of the trail leads through an ancient apple orchard, where dozens of trees blossom midspring. Next, the trail plunges into a mixed old-growth forest, mainly maple and beech, with some trees that rarely grow this far north, such as the shagbark and bitternut hickories. The undergrowth is sparse, giving a very open feeling.

The third ecosystem is the wetter area on the edge of the bay. Here water-loving silver maple grow, on roots like craggy stilts. Not much farther along is the highlight of the trail: an unpainted wooden boardwalk leading for several hundred metres across the marsh. In spring there are clear views of the bay; later, the walkway becomes a green corridor through the tall reeds.

At the end of the boardwalk is a two-storey observation tower. With a good pair of binoculars you should have no trouble spotting the giant nests of the Great Heron colony on the bay's far shore, especially in early spring, when there are no leaves on the trees. There are usually about 90 nests.

For a shortcut to the observation tower and boardwalk, take the right-hand fork just past the orchard, against the flow of pedestrian traffic.

Farther into the park is the **Oka Calvary** trail, a route dating to 1721, when the first European settlement, a mission, was established in Oka. Between 1740 and 1742, the church and converts built 7 of the 14 traditional Stations of the Cross along a lovely wooded trail leading to the summit of Calvary Mountain.

In 1869 most Indians in Oka left the church over land disputes, and the annual pilgrimage was opened to Montrealers. The beauty of the river trip and the Oka countryside made it a huge success. Dozens of steamboats set off from Montreal, Lachine and Ste Anne de Bellevue each autumn. In 1899, 30,000 people participated, though most of the men opted to drink and socialize at the base of mountain. The following year the pilgrimage was cancelled.

Over 250 years later, the four humble oratories and three diminutive chapels still stand along the trail and at the summit of the mountain. The oratories are small wood, fieldstone and stucco buildings set in the tall maple-beech-birch old-growth forest of the mountainside. The chapels are at the summit, between an oak forest and a wonderful view. There are picnic tables at the top, though the only toilets are at the base of the trail.

The packed-earth trails make a mainly easy hike of about 5.5 km, with some challenges, particularly in the final 30 m. Pick up a (French) pamphlet at the visitor's centre or start of the trail since the trails are poorly marked. Follow the direction indicated in the pamphlet for a gentle hike up, with a steeper descent.

2020 Chemin d'Oka
(450) 479-8365

Season and Hours
Park: 8 a.m.–8 p.m. daily.
Visitor's centre: 9 a.m.–4 p.m. Mon–Fri, 8 a.m.–6 p.m. weekends. Calvary Trail toilets: 8 a.m.–8 p.m. daily.

Fees
Free.

Directions
Take Highway 15 (Laurentian Autoroute) north to Highway 640. Follow the 640 to the end (it leads into the park). For a shortcut to Calvary Mountain, turn right where Highway 640 ends, onto Route 344.

27

Cap St Jacques
Nature Park

C ap St Jacques, on a wide peninsula pushing out into the Lake of Two Mountains, is the largest, most diverse and most remote of the MUC nature parks. Surrounded by water on three sides, it has 27 km of trails for hiking and skiing, a huge beach and a working farm. It even has a summer camp. This is the only nature park with absolutely no urban infrastructures within its borders: no electrical towers, train tracks or highways. As a result, it is the one park on the island that feels thoroughly like the country.

Grassy picnic areas—five large and several smaller ones—stretch out along the waterside walking trails. There is no shortage of fine views. The nicest is from l'Embouchure (the Mouth) on the park's north shore. There's barely a house in sight, in a panorama that overlooks the lake, the Rivière des Prairies and Oka in the distance. Each picnic area has dry toilets and coal disposal for barbecues. Most are served by small parking lots.

The maple forest in the park's interior is quite enormous. It is a great spot for a ramble through the autumn leaves, and even more popular in winter, when cross-country skiers hit the rolling trails. It is distinguished by the natural state of its packed-earth paths and its mixed deciduous forest typical of the lower Laurentians. There is a nature-interpretation trail designed for kids, but the panels don't provide an awful lot of information.

Hidden deep in the forest is a quaint sugar shack. Each spring a horse and carriage brings visitors here to watch the maple sap boil and enjoy other related activities. On winter weekends this is a great place to warm up, since delicious, inexpensive pancakes and coffee are served.

On the park's north shoreline is the Eco-Farm, a full-sized working farm with two barns and a greenhouse open to visitors. A gorgeous vegetable garden is planted in wide arcs, and the horses, pigs, highland cows, chickens, goats and other animals are beautifully kept. There is another large picnic area here, and a restaurant serves the farm's fresh produce.

Cap St Jacques is well known for its public beach, a wide swath of fine white sand on the Lake of Two Mountains. On summer weekends this popular beach turns into a mini-Cape Cod (though quieter, since radios are not permitted). As at most beaches on the lake, the water is shallow—1.5 m at its deepest. While getting to the beach still requires a 750 m walk for those arriving by public transport, a new parking lot gives easy access to the sands for those coming by car.

A second, smaller beach is reserved for the use of the camp, a tent city that can be booked by groups. Over 3,000 children and teens a year take advantage of this great setting.

When you venture into the park in winter, the wind off the lake can be chilly. Dress warmly even if only heading into the woods, since you must cross a large open field. If you look forward to cycling, head to nearby Bois de l'Île Bizard (page 76) or Bois de Liesse (page 86) instead; almost all the trails at Cap St Jacques are off limits to bikes.

20,099 Gouin Blvd West (Pierrefonds)
Visitor's centre
(514) 280-6871
Eco-Farm
(514) 280-6743
Château Gohier (near beach)
(514) 620-4025
MUC Nature Parks Info Line
(514) 280-PARC (7272)

For hours, fees and directions, see page 141.

28

Bois de
l'Île Bizard
Nature Park

H ere's a park that's perfect for cycling. Its packed-earth trails lead through forests and fields, crossing footbridges, boardwalks and streams. They vary in width and have just the right number of dips and rises to make them interesting. In the park's deepest reaches, you find yourself in an open forest with the canopy high overhead. But there are trails to the edge of the back river, too, and through short open stretches that are delightful in the sun.

Like our national parks, Bois de l'Île Bizard nature park is divided into a recreation area and a conservation area. The recreational part is at the north end, on the Lake of Two Mountains. Pointe aux Carrières is where you'll find the largest parking lot, the visitor's centre and the beach. The brand-new visitor's centre has a distinctly nautical look. It houses a snack bar, toilets and information desk. You can rent kayaks, canoes or pedalboats to explore the quieter bays, or bicycles for the conservation area.

The tiny beach is never crowded, and since the water is very shallow, it is ideal for a paddle with the kids. The sand is fine, and the slope is gentle. The water quality is analysed weekly, as it is at all beaches on the Lake of Two Mountains. Call ahead if you plan to swim.

In an effort to discourage seagulls, eating isn't allowed on the sand, but on the eastern edge of the beach a long, grassy peninsula juts out into the lake. Recently landscaped and shady, this is the park's official picnic area. There's a wonderful wooden gazebo overlooking the lake and beach. It is also a great place to take in a sunset, but don't forget insect repellent—at dusk the mosquitoes are fierce.

The conservation area across the road to the south is much larger than the recreational part. Don't let the dreary appearance of the first bit of the path discourage you. It opens quite suddenly onto a huge marsh, with a fantastic wooden boardwalk. It is the nicest, longest boardwalk in the region, wide enough for cycling side by side, with room left over for passing. It curves across the marsh for over half a kilometre. The ducks and other waterfowl aren't shy, sometimes nesting very near the boardwalk.

At the far end of the marsh, the path enters a wonderful cedar forest, crosses a second smaller marsh and joins the park's central region. In the lightly wooded area just south of the boardwalk, keep your eyes open for the Eastern Bluebird. Only 14 nests have been recorded in Montreal, and the park is proud that a number of pairs have been seen nesting here. The central part of the park is roughly triangular in shape, crisscrossed by very well-maintained trails. Most of the trees are old, though some paths pass through what is clearly newer growth.

One path worth exploring—Secteur les Rapides, on the signposts—leads to the rapids between Île Bizard and Laval. The waterfront area is not very pretty, but the current in this narrow channel is impressive, and you can often see pleasure boats struggling upriver.

There is a third route into the park from Église St, but the scenery isn't much to speak of.

2115 Chemin Bord du Lac
Visitor's centre: (514) 280-8517;
MUC park info line: (514) 280-6766.

Season and Hours

Park: All year, sunrise to sunset. Visitor's centre: May 1–Oct 31: 10 a.m.–5 p.m. (7 p.m. in summer). Beach: Mid-June–third weekend Aug: 10:30 a.m.–5 p.m. (7 p.m. on weekends).

Fees

Park free. Parking $4 per day (25¢, $1, $2, Visa or MasterCard; dispensers at Pointe aux Carrières entrance only). Bike rental (May 1–Oct 31) $5/hr, $7/2 hr $9/3 hr, $15/6 hr. Canoe, kayak, pedalboat rental (June 24–Labour Day, weekends only) $8/hr, $18/3 hr, $24/6 hr.

Directions

Car: Take Highway 20 or Highway 40, then go north on St John's Blvd. Head west on Pierrefonds Blvd West, then north on Jacques Bizard Blvd onto Île Bizard. Turn left on Cherrier, then go north on de l'Église. At Bord du Lac turn right. Bus: Orange line to Côte Vertu. Take the 144 bus to the ferry on Laval. Take the ferry to Île Bizard. Turn left and go 500 m to entrance, or cycle along Bord du Lac north to the visitor's centre.

29

Year-Round Beauty at the
Morgan Arboretum
Ste Anne de Bellevue

Photo: John Watson

I n the late 19th century, retailing mogul James Morgan of Morgan's department store fame (now The Bay) consolidated 21 farm lots straddling Ste Anne de Bellevue and Senneville, on the western tip of the island. On weekends, friends of the family would take the train to St Anne's, then picnic or ride on 245 ha of pristine fields and woodlands. The trains are gone, and horses rarely seen, but Canada's largest arboretum lives on, and it is open to visitors all year long.

Since its acquisition by McGill University in 1945—partly purchased by the university and partly donated by the Morgan family—the arboretum has been dedicated to the preservation of trees and shrubs (*arbor* is Latin for tree). In fact, the arboretum was the first tree farm in Quebec, certified in 1953. For over 50 years, staff and volunteers have been planting and tending, with remarkable results. The area now boasts 150 species of trees and shrubs and over 350 species of smaller plants.

It is not just the variety of growth, but the way it is laid out, that makes a walk through the arboretum a treat, any time of year. As you stroll the wide, well-maintained paths, you pass through 20 separate collections of trees. One moment, you're in an apple orchard, the next, an open field. A few

DEC/MAR

steps later, you'll pass by row upon row of birch trees. An especially interest-ing stretch is the spruce, cedar and juniper forest set in a glen. In gardens these trees are usually neatly trimmed; here they have an untamed look, like a topiary garden gone wild. Many trees are clearly identified.

The arboretum's maple stands, with trees over 200 years old, are some of Montreal's last remaining virgin forest; the Bois de Liesse Nature Park has the only other uncut woods on the island. There is also plenty of secondary growth well over a century old.

In the warm season, something is always blooming: apple trees or rose bushes, magnolias or lilacs, or simply wildflowers in fields. For picnickers, there are tables near the conservation centre, which has toilets and a snack bar.

For a self-guided tour, pick up a booklet and make tracks. Two Forest Management trails (1.2 km and 1.8 km) offer interesting insights into the forces that affect a forest's growth. The Ecology Trail (2 km) brings you closer to the ferns and microhabitats of one of the wetter parts of the arboretum.

In winter, the arboretum keeps 20 km of trails open for use, including 7 km of groomed cross-country ski trails (mainly easy). A kilometre and a half of the central road is kept ploughed for walking.

The arboretum hosts a number of special weekends throughout the year. In mid-December the conservation centre turns into a gift shop for a day, selling high-quality locally made crafts. Christmas trees are also sold throughout the month.

In early March, Springfest features a whole host of activities for all ages. The prize-winning Macdonald Woodsmen put on a show that includes cross-cut sawing, bow sawing, horizontal and vertical chop-ping, and axe throwing. In the afternoon, children are invited to participate in friendly, safe young woodsman competitions.

Keep an eye out for the sugaring-off open house later in March. Watch the sap boil or feast on *tourtière* (meat pie), baked beans and other traditional fare.

150 Chemin des Pins
(514) 398-7812

Season and Hours
9 a.m.–4 p.m., every day, all year. Members only on winter weekends.

Fees
Adults $5, children 5 and up $2, under 5 free, family $12.

Directions
Take Highway 40 (Trans-Canada) west to exit 41 (Ste Anne de Bellevue). Continue west on Ste Marie Rd. Turn left on Chemin des Pins (Pine Rd).

30

Caribou and Timber Wolves
at the Ecomuseum
Ste Anne de Bellevue

Photo: Estelle Bolker

The Ecomuseum is Montreal's own "Field of Dreams." In 1965, McGill University's Roger Bider visited the Arizona Sierra Museum, where desert wildlife resides in ecologically designed enclosures, the goal of which is to encourage preservation of the animals' natural habitats. The idea stayed with him, and in the early '80s he began shifting earth on an old landfill and dump on the West Island. He got a helping hand when, as soon as the first enclosure was built, a man brought him two orphaned bear cubs. What could he do? He offered the bears a home. Dr Bider built it, and they came.

The bears are still there, and they've been joined by caribou, wolves, arctic foxes, raccoons, skunks, porcupines, coyotes, otters, deer, lynx, snakes, turtles—the list is impressive. The Ecomuseum has succeeded in its goal of representing the major species of wildlife native to the St Lawrence Valley. It has over 40 species in all, housed in almost two dozen environments, nicely arranged along comfortable walking paths.

The Ecomuseum is a wildlife observation centre, not a zoo: the key difference lies in its educational role. That said, it's too bad more zoos aren't like the Ecomuseum. Most of the enclosures are large and were designed with the needs of the animals in mind. In addition, the animals are allowed to follow their natural rhythms. If you visit in winter, for example, you won't see the bears, because they'll be hibernating. And while porcupines and raccoons don't hibernate, they do hide out during the colder months. No attempt is made to convince them to do otherwise.

One highlight is the walk-in aviary. Over 14 species of waterfowl and other birds fly freely under a huge net canopy. A boardwalk leads through various habitats, including a marshy area where some birds nest and a pretty stand of sumac and cedar. The raven and crow enclosure always draws a crowd. These clever birds are real talkers and seem to love human attention.

Wolves used to be common in the St Lawrence Valley, and the Ecomuseum has two beautiful animals. The male is larger and is pure timber wolf. The female is of mixed breed—part timber wolf, Siberian wolf and dog.

The Ecomuseum also has an impressive assortment of birds of prey, acquired when it absorbed part of the McGill raptor centre. These are injured birds that could not survive in the wild. Most of them sit on top of their doghouse-style homes, tethered to a wire that allows them to fly to a perch.

One habitat often overlooked—probably due to its bunker-like entrance—is the experimental fish pond. It's worth the trip down the damp concrete staircase for a mud-puppy's-eye view of life in a pond. This pond is left to its own devices, so actually seeing any fish can be a challenge. In winter, the algae die, so the water is much clearer.

There are two special events at the Ecomuseum. On Easter weekend, the staff hides hundreds of clothespegs, which can be traded in for chocolate. On the last weekend in October, it's time for Chuck-a-Duck Day. Injured ducks are often brought to the museum to be nursed back to health and on this day you bid for the privilege of releasing one back into the wild.

21,125 Chemin Ste Marie
(514) 457-9449
Season and Hours
9 a.m.–5 p.m., every day, year round. Closed Christmas and New Year's.
Fees
Adults $5, children 5–12 $3, under 5 free.
Directions
Take Highway 40 (Trans-Canada) west to exit 44 (Morgan Blvd). Turn left at the stop sign and continue west on Ste Marie Rd to the Ecomuseum entrance, on the right-hand side.

The Udderly Amazing
Macdonald Farm
Ste Anne de Bellevue

Ask a classroom of city kids if milk comes out of a cow warm or cold, and dollars to doughnuts someone will get it wrong. It's understandable. Most city children haven't seen a cow up close, though it's a problem that's easy to fix. McGill University has about 648 ha of farmland under cultivation on the West Island, and keeps pigs, sheep, and dairy cows on the 100 ha between highways 20 and 40. You can visit the dairy cows on your own, or for a real education go with a guide. And though it's a university farm, there's no quiz at the end of the tour!

Visits begin just outside the farm office, where a dozen or so calves spend their first few months in pens that look like giant white doghouses. These friendly little animals love to be petted. If one tries to suck on your finger or thumb, don't worry, they haven't any teeth (though they sure know how to drool). Cows need to give birth before they can be milked, so there are always calves around the farm, and it's not uncommon for visitors to see one being born.

Dairy farms normally raise just one kind of cow, but at Macdonald the herd is almost as multicultural as Montreal. There are about 60 cows of three breeds: Holsteins, Ayrshires and Jerseys. The black and white Holsteins are good low-fat milk producers. Ayrshires, about the same size, have patches of red or brown with white. They produce less milk but are hardier. Jerseys are brown and slightly smaller than the other two, and produce a milk high in fat. The milk you get in a carton is always a mix of all three kinds, with the fat—also known as cream—skimmed off for other uses.

Each cow has a name, though their ear tags show just a number and date of birth. Keep an eye out for Pépite (number 993); she was in one of Carmen Campagne's videos. Stardom hasn't affected her, though, and she still produces 40 or so litres of milk a day, like other good cows. You might notice that none of the cows has horns. Cows do grow horns naturally, but they are clipped when the calves are a couple of months old.

The cows are milked three times a day, at 4:30 a.m., 11:30 a.m. and 7:30 p.m. (up from the traditional twice daily). Even if you miss the milking, you can follow the stainless-steel pipes to the 9,000 L tank in the milk room. This room also contains the world's biggest baby bottle, for feeding the calves.

Another tour highlight is the area where the heifers (young cows) are kept. Don't forget to pile onto the cow scale to see if your group weighs as much as a cow. A full-grown Holstein weighs 530–710 kg.

The older stone barn across the road doesn't contain livestock anymore; it houses a collection of antique farm equipment. Not much is labelled and you can't get very close, but most things don't need much explanation.

In tour season (mid-May to September) be sure to visit the show ring, the taller hexagonal building on the end of the old barn. This bright, airy room holds a petting zoo, with lambs, ducks, geese, exotic chickens and even a couple of llamas.

21,111 Lakeshore Rd.
(514) 398-7701
Reservations required for group tours.

Season and Hours
Office: Mon–Fri 8 a.m.–8 p.m.
Visits: 11:30 a.m.–3 p.m. daily.
Guided tours: Mon–Fri 9 a.m.–5 p.m., mid-May–Sept.

Fees
Visit: Free. Guided tour: $3 per person, minimum 10 people.

Directions
Highway 40 (Trans-Canada) to exit 41 (Ste Anne de Bellevue), then onto Ste Marie Rd. Turn right at first stop sign and left at the second. Cross over the highway via the overpass. The farm office entrance is on the right.

Tilting at Windmills at
Pointe du Moulin
Île Perrot

Y ou know you're
on the way to
Windmill Point
when you turn onto
Don Quichotte (Don
Quixote) Blvd. Once
past the surfeit of car
dealerships, it is easy enough to imagine a donkey-riding knight clip-clop-
ping along this lovely country road to the windmill. The delightful little
park on the southern tip of the island has walking paths, two picnic areas,
a visitor's centre, and, of course, an old windmill.

As you enter the park, you pass through one of the nicest visitor's centres to be found. The wood-shingled buildings are an architectural surprise—they appear to have been been divided in half and separated to
make way for the path. Inside are a snack bar, toilets and a water cooler.
You might want to fill up before venturing out into the park, since water is
not always available farther along.

There is a small exhibtion on early farming practices, and children can
dip their hands into buckets of wheat, barley, oats and buckwheat.

A scale model of the windmill's inner works occupies a large part of one
room. Children will enjoy tossing in sandbags that look like grain. Next, a
staff member turns on the windmill, and out comes "flour." Finally, kids

can sift the ground grain to separate the larger bits from the smaller.

A short walk through some very nice woods—there is also a trail with panels explaining plants and animals of interest—leads to a shaded point of land with a grassy area. The miller's house is worth a visit, especially on Sunday afternoons, when bread is baked the old-fashioned way in a wood-fired brick oven. Samples are served.

Right next door is the windmill, dating from 1708. It is one of two still operational in the province of Quebec (the other is on Île aux Coudres, near Quebec City). Due to the age of the windmill, its sails aren't set in motion too often—the wind has to be just right—and it is only on the occasional Sunday that you will see it working.

Working or not, it is a remarkable construction. The roof is a heavy wooden structure weighing about 5 t. Despite its weight, it can be rotated so that the sails will pick up the wind. This is why, like most windmills, it has two doors—it allows the miller a means of entering and exiting no matter which side the sails are on. As a note of interest, when a miller forgot and left through the wrong door, the windmill was dubbed a *"moulin rouge"* (red windmill) after the unfortunate accident that ensued.

Also noteworthy are the rectangular holes in the windmill's walls, a couple of metres off the ground. While it appears as if bricks or floor beams have fallen out, in reality these are loopholes, through which weapons could be fired.

Defending a mill may seem a bit odd, but there is some question as to whether the windmill ever actually ground much grain. Seigneur Perrot, the rumour goes, was actually a big dealer in the illegal fur trade, intercepting canoes on their way to Montreal, both by bribe and by force. This earned him enemies on both sides of the trading counter and resulted in what may be the world's only defendable windmill. Tilt your lance at that one, Don Quixote.

2500 boul. Don Quixote
(514) 453-5936
Season and Hours
9 a.m.–5 p.m., weekdays, mid-May–June 24; 10 a.m.–6 p.m.,weekends; daily 10 a.m.–6 p.m., June 24–end Aug; weekends 12 p.m.–5 p.m., Labour Day–Thanksgiving.
Fees
Free.
Directions
Take Highway 20 west to Île Perrot. Once on the island, turn south on Don Quichotte Blvd and follow it to the end.

Fields, Streams
and Hardwood Forests at
Bois de Liesse
Nature Park

Think of Pierrefonds, Dollard des Ormeaux or Ville St Laurent, and deep woods probably aren't the first image that springs to mind. Yet if you take the time to explore Bois de Liesse Nature Park, which straddles these three districts, that's just what you'll find. Not only does it have one of the deepest, greenest, forests on the island, it also includes fields, marshland and one of Montreal's last open streams. You'll also find great cycling and walking paths, a couple of visitor's centres and serviceable picnic areas.

At 159 ha the park is about the size of Mount Royal. Like the other MUC nature parks, it is very clean and well managed, with perfectly maintained paths. In summer it has 8 km of trails for cycling and 12 km for walking (some shared with cyclists), in three distinct areas: the Fields, Peninsula and Bois Francs (hardwood forest). The three are connected by trails, and each area has its own parking lot with ticket dispenser.

The most popular entrance is just off Gouin Blvd, east of Highway 13. In visitor's centre, Pitfield House, there are a snack bar, washrooms and a few exhibits. Pick up a map—you'll need it unless you don't mind getting lost—or rent a bike there.

The main path in the nearby Peninsula area follows the edge of meandering Betrand Creek to the Rivière des Prairies (the back river). This messy-looking creek is one of the last open streams on the island. It widens in two places, and there are several nice lookouts along its banks. One extends over the water, where you'll almost certainly see ducks, herons and beaver lodges.

Wide biking and walking paths edged with fieldstones wind through the Fields, south of Gouin Blvd from Pitfield house. Some fields have been mowed while others are left to themselves, so there are lots of butterflies, birds and wildflowers, in season. The visitor's centre in this area is a modern building, half buried, strangely enough, in a small artificial hill. It houses an information counter and tables, and is the focus for a large picnic area.

The Bois Francs is the largest and most spectacular of the three areas. If you only have time or energy for one area, this is a good choice. While initially the walk from the Fields parking lot might seem rather dull, keep going. You will soon find yourself in an extraordinary maple-beech forest.

A wide log-edged path leads through the rippled terrain carpeted with ferns. Some of the trees are over 100 years old, including specimens of the rare black maple. In spring the forest floor lights up when thousands upon thousands of snow white trilliums bloom. When the trees are in full leaf and the sunlight streams in, the forest glows an emerald green.

A number of paths lead off the main route. One of these is a short excursion alongside a railway line through a marshy area where tall reeds grow. Another—very pretty—is a Japanese-style boardwalk, several feet off the wettest part of the forest floor. In the densest part of the forest, the land dips, and a deep woodsy smell emanates from the moist central area.

Note: In spring and summer, the park is popular with mosquitoes, too!

9432 Gouin Blvd West
Pitfield House (bike rental)
(514) 280-6729
Fields area visitor's centre
(514) 280-6678
Peninsula area discovery house
(514) 280-6829
MUC Nature Parks Info Line
(514) 280-PARC (7272)

For hours, fees and directions, see page 142.

The Fur Trade Museum in Lachine

F or 300 years, hats were the fashion in Europe, and felt hats were the most popular of all. As a result, throughout the 17th, 18th and 19th centuries, Europe's stocks of fur-bearing wildlife dwindled. When Canada was colonized by the French, it became the main source of supply.

Why the beaver? First of all, Canadian beavers grow very thick fur in response to the cold climate. Furthermore beaver fur felts exceptionally well. It is the short, downy hairs close to the skin that are used to make felt. If you look at the "down" under a microscope you'll see it has a scaly surface, with terrifically jagged edges. Under steam and pressure, these edges lock together, like Velcro. Beaver down locks together best.

A small fieldstone building on edge of Lachine Canal is all that remains of the fur trade in Montreal. It was built by a former clerk of the North West Company in 1803, when about 80% of furs passed through a few such warehouses. We owe its preservation to the Grey Nuns, who for many years used it as a residence. It opened as a museum in 1984.

The fur trade is a story of big business, cultural exchange and the eventual death of the traditional Indian way of life. But it also the story of the voyageurs. These young men from Sorel, Three Rivers and other towns met the Native trappers on their own turf, trading manufactured goods for pelts.

In 1777, at just about the height of the fur trade, some 2,500 voyageurs were registered in Montreal and Detroit. Probably twice this many were active that year, from Montreal to the Rockies, Hudson Bay to the Gulf of Mexico.

The voyageurs' means of transportation was the birchbark canoe; there is one hanging in the rafters at the museum. The enormous canoes were designed to hold 10 men and 60 bundles of fur, for a total charge of 1,500 kg. On a cedar frame, with pine-root lashing, pine sap chinking and bark covering, they were fragile, but everything needed for repairs could be found en route.

Being a voyageur was prestigious and it paid well—about three times the wage of a farm hand. But the men worked like devils. They paddled 16–18 hours a day, with a mere five-minute break each hour to smoke a pipe of tobacco. The pace was a brisk 60 strokes a minute, and to keep time, the men sang the spirited songs still familiar today.

The museum explains the origins of the "*ceinture fléchée*," the colourful woven belts of the French pioneers. During portages (a word given to us by the voyageurs), the men carried two bales at a time, or 81 kg—a considerable load for one who tipped the scale himself at no more than 63 kg and was at most 178 cm tall. The *ceinture fléchée*, then, was actually a compression belt, serving the same purpose as those used by modern weightlifters. (The two leading causes of death amongst the Voyageurs were drowning and herniation.)

There are no guided tours, but staff are on hand to answer questions. Interactive displays illustrate the history of the trade nicely: A map lights up to show the hundreds of trading posts and you can measure and weigh yourself see if you'd qualify to be a voyageur. On Sunday afternoons from June 24–Labour Day, the museum has walking tours of the canal area or demonstrations of felt hatmaking, depending on the weather. The museum grounds are a marvellous spot for a picnic.

1255 St Joseph
(514) 637-7433
Season and Hours
Apr 1–mid-Nov: 1 p.m.–6 p.m. Mon, 10 a.m.–6 p.m. Tue–Sun.
Fees
Adults $2.50, students and youth 6–16 $1.25, family $6.25.
Directions
Green line to Angrignon, 195 bus to St Louis and 12th Ave. Walk south on 12th one block.

Laval

⚙ Quebec's second largest city is also its second largest island, a shade smaller than Montreal, but considerably more rural. About a third of the island (actually named Île Jésus) is given over to agricultural use, and Laval is the province's largest producer of both corn *and* cut flowers,

oddly enough. L'Orée des Bois park is totally unspoiled and has an out-of-town feel. In fact you are quite likely to find yourself alone on its riverside trails and boardwalks. The more central Boisé Papineau is another nature escape that you

might well have all to yourself. ❂ The Laval Nature
Centre is more civilized. It is
much like Mount Royal Park
near Beaver Lake, with a
barn, greenhouse and white-
tailed deer in the mix.

On the science side of the
ledger, Laval has two attractions of note. The
slick Cosmodome puts the emphasis on space
exploration and telecommunications. On Laval's
north shore is a virtual shrine to one of Quebec's
most renowned researchers, Dr Armand
Frappier. ❂ But the jewel in Laval's crown is the
Parc de la Rivière des Milles Îles. It's a gorgeous
park, with a twist: If you want to stroll its many
woodland paths, you'll have to do some paddling
first! Its 30 or so islands are tailor-made for a
canoeing adventure.

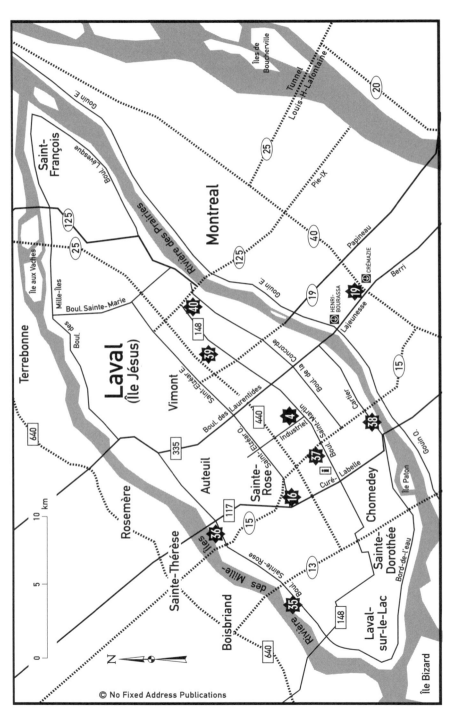

TRIP DESTINATIONS
(denoted by star symbol on map)

35. L'Orée des Bois Park
37th Ave and Mille Îles River
(450) 978-8904
p. 94

36. Mille Îles River Regional Park
345 Ste Rose Blvd
(450) 622-1020
p. 96

37. Cosmodome
2150 Highway 15 (Laurentian
Autoroute)
(450) 978-3600
p. 98

38. Armand Frappier Museum
531 Des Prairies Blvd
(450) 686-5641
p. 100

39. Boisé Papineau
3235 St Martin East
(450) 662-7610 or (450) 662-4901
p. 102

40. Laval Nature Centre
54 Parc
(450) 662-4942
p. 104

4. F1 Indoor Karting
1755 Fortin
(450) 829-2121
p. 18

16. Action Directe
4377 St Elzéar West
(450) 688-0515
p. 44

TOURIST INFORMATION

Laval Tourist Office
2900 St Martin West
(450) 682-5522, 1 800 463-3765

Laval Recreation Department (Fabreville)
(450) 978-8904

Laval Recreation Department (Duvernay)
(450) 662-4901

Société de Transport de Laval (bus)
(450) 688-6520

Laval–Île Bizard ferry
(450) 627-2526

Riverside
Boardwalks
in l'Orée des Bois

Approaching l'Orée des Bois park in the Fabreville region of Laval, you might tend to feel slightly disappointed. No signposts point the way, and the streets seem a little too residential and well planned to conceal much of anything. But when you see the giant Bavarian-looking homestead at the end of the street on the river's edge, you start to think, hmm, this just might be uncharted territory. A few minutes into the park, from atop its first boardwalk-bridge overlooking the Mille Îles River, the decision comes in: Laval has done it again. L'Orée des Bois—literally the Wood's Edge—is a great little park, with an authentic ruggedness you don't often find so near the city.

You can enter the park in a couple of places: by the high school of the same name that marks its southern limit, or by a boat ramp, where there is room for a few cars to park.

Try the boat ramp entrance, simply for the pleasure of seeing the homestead that looks as if it was lifted straight out of a German fairy tale. The main house and large outbuildings have painted exposed beams and white stucco walls. But this is the dream home of a gentleman who moved here from France 30 years ago, and the influence is Norman-Alsatian. There is a small apple orchard and a lilac tree on the grounds, plus lots of ornamentation, including a traditional weathercock.

Chances are you'll have the packed-earth footpaths and basic boardwalks of this 8 ha park all to yourself. There is no visitor's centre, no toilets and just one picnic table. It seems to be a park for those in the know. Despite the lack of supervision, it is extremely clean, and local residents and the high-school students clearly have a lot of respect for the secret treasure in their midst.

There are no maps of the park, nor any signs to help you on your way, but you are unlikely to need any. There are just 1.5 km of easy walking trails: one great loop along the river's edge, intersected by a couple of smaller paths, and one or two that lead away from the river to the back of the school. All are worth exploring, though you will probably find yourself doubling back once or twice, since it is easy to take a wrong turn and end up on a "personal" path leading to a backyard. For a lovely view of the river, head down the dead-end path to the water's edge.

The riverside portion of the park is quite low-lying, so a fair portion of it consists of wetlands (though not marsh) and land that floods in the spring. Tall silver maples grow along the shore, and bright green ferns of all kinds populate the inner reaches. Bridges and boardwalks keep your feet dry.

Beyond the wetlands is an older growth beech and maple stand with an open view of the forest floor. In spring it is carpeted in trilliums of all kinds: white, pink and white, and, more rarely, pink. On higher ground you will find delicate purple, white and yellow violets. Be forewarned that later in the season, mosquito repellent is a must.

37th Ave and Mille Îles River
Bureau Municipale des Loisirs
(Fabreville): (450) 978-8904

Season and Hours
Mid-April–Sept: 7 a.m.–10 p.m.;
Oct–mid-April: 7 a.m.–7 p.m.

Fees
Free.

Directions
Orange line to Henri Bourassa. Take the 72 bus to Ste Rose Blvd and 37th Ave. Walk north on 37th Ave to entrance.

36

Life Is But a Dream
at the Mille Îles
River Regional Park

Montreal is so big, it's easy to forget it's an island. In fact, there are about 250 islands in the waters around Montreal and Île Jesus (Laval) and in just the narrow strip separating the north shore of Laval from Boisbriand and Rosemere there is an archipelago of 30 or so islands. Thanks to the Mille Îles River Regional Park, this precious cluster is now being carefully preserved, and a 10 km stretch of river is also open for visits—provided you don't mind paddling a bit!

To get out there, you can rent a variety of watercraft. There are three or four kinds of kayaks, canoes, rowboats or pedalboats for fooling around on the "inner channels." In a big gang? Consider renting a 20-seat *rabaska* canoe, modelled after those used by the voyageurs.

A beautiful pamphlet (in French only) with an old-fashioned style presents four self-guided tours. Islands, highlights and landing points are clearly indicated, both on the map and by corresponding signposts on the water. There are 10 islands where you can disembark, with about 10 km of hiking trails. No special athletic ability is required, since there is almost no current.

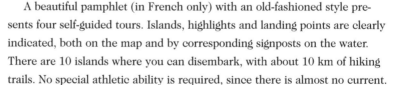

At 4.8 km, the Tournée du Grand Duc (Grand Duke's Voyage) is the shortest and most popular trip, taking a leisurely couple of hours to complete. Nearby Kennedy Island is the first stop (you can paddle to it in about 10 minutes.) It has half a dozen picnic tables, dry toilets and water (bring your own cup).

A few minutes later, you reach the narrow passage between Île aux

Fraises (Strawberry Island) and Île des Juifs (Jews' Island). You're sure to see a beaver or two here, and a signpost marks the watery grave of a wrecked barge, just a few centimetres beneath the surface.

Jews' Island is the largest of the park's islands. Strolling the path that leads around its edge, you'll find red oak, white cedar, ironwood, floodwater-loving silver maple and enormous evergreens (two over 100 years old). Keep an eye out for the red crown of the giant Pileated Woodpecker. This island also has an abandoned cabin.

The Bout du Monde (End of the World) is a longer trip (9.5 km), but less interesting, since most the course follows densely populated islands near Rosemere, with few interesting-looking houses. Still, the Boisbriand Nature Centre, the turn-around point, seems like a nice place for a lunch and there is some marshland along the way.

The Repaire du Diable (Devil's Den) is another gem. You'll travel under Highway 15 and through a wide channel before arriving at a huge marsh pressing in on a large bay. A two-storey floating observation tower moored here makes a great spot for a picnic or a rest. The Histoire Perdue (Lost History) trail takes you downstream to the shores of Rosemere, then back through the narrow channel of a watery forest.

The park also offers guided tours in a 30-seat *rabaska*, led by a guide in historic garb. And if you don't feel up to paddling, you can take a two-hour boat tour of all the islands, departing from the nearby Venice marina.

Tips: Wear sunscreen, a hat and insect repellent, and bring plenty to drink. Gardening gloves are useful, since paddling can make your hands quite dirty.

345 Ste Rose Blvd
(4 blocks east of Highway 15)
(450) 622-1020

Season and Hours
Park: Mid-May, Jun, Sept: 9 a.m.–6 p.m.; Jul–Aug: 9 a.m.–10 p.m. Last rental 1 hr before closing. Guided theatrical *rabaska* tours: Tues–Sun 7 p.m. Boat tour from marina: 1:30 p.m., 4 p.m. daily, June; 10 a.m., 1:30 p.m., 4 p.m., 6 p.m. daily, July–Aug.

Fees
Park: Free. Canoe: $8/hr, $25/day, $110/wk; kayak: $7/hr, $25/day, $110/wk; two-seat kayak: $12/hr, $40/day, $130/wk; pedalboat or rowboat: $9/hr, $35/day, $120/wk; *rabaska*: $20/hr, $80/day, $350/wk. Photo ID required. Guided theatrical *rabaska* tours (minimum 6 adults): Adults $23, children under 12 $4, students and seniors $19. Marina: Adults $12, students and seniors $10, 6–12 $6, family $63.

Directions
Orange line to Henri Bourassa. STL (Societé de Transport de Laval) bus 72 to park entrance.

37

To Infinity and Beyond at the
Cosmodome

Photo: Laval Tourism Bureau

When you pass through the sliding doors of Laval's Cosmodome, you enter a world beyond time and space. The lighting is space-station subdued, and guides in NASA blue jumpsuits greet you at the door. Though similar to Ottawa's Science Centre, the Cosmodome focusses exclusively on the history of aerospace, telecommunications and computer science. Space noises, push buttons, holograms and computer graphics abound in this museum, making it a blend of science centre, video game and amusement park.

The museum features truly beautiful scale models of various missiles and rockets—including a full-sized replica of the world's first satellite, *Sputnik*—as well as astronomically inspired historic sites such as Stonehenge and Mayan temples, with detailed explanations of the cosmological reasons behind their designs.

One area features a model of our own solar system, with a huge glowing demihemisphere of the sun on one wall. Each planet is to scale and is surrounded by a shallow well showing what its surface is believed to look like. Earth's has ferns growing in it, for example, while Venus's is charred by sulphuric acid. The wells of the four gas giants—Jupiter, Saturn, Uranus and Neptune—feature dry-ice mist floating up from the base.

But while the size of the planets is to scale, the distance between them is not: If Montreal were the sun, Earth and Mars would be near Ottawa, Pluto would be in Vancouver and Uranus would be somewhere near Winnipeg. A video screen by each planet presents the facts, and high-resolution computer animation simulates a trip across the planet's surface.

Sound doesn't travel in a vacuum, and at the Cosmodome they offer proof. One of the hands-on displays features a bell ringing inside a glass chamber. When you press a button, the air is sucked out of the chamber, and the ringing fades away.

Another display explains the nature of satellite communication. You speak into a parabolic dish. The sound travels through air upwards to another dish—the "satellite"—where it is carried by wire to another, then back down through air to the receiving parabolic dish.

Don't skip the superb 360-degree multimedia show that combines film, slides, holographic projections and 3,500 optical fibres to present a history of human interest in the cosmos. While the acting is a little hokey, the show is informative, entertaining and a technological wonder in itself. The holographic projections are so real you can almost feel the flames as the library of Alexandria burns. In another scene, Newton dances gleefully while apples swarm around him like planets. It's difficult to determine what's real and what isn't, as the 100-seat theatre tilts, rotates, rises and descends to various scenes, with incredible *trompe l'oeil* sets.

The Cosmodome also runs a space camp, which is open to the public several times a year. You'll get the chance to be tossed and turned by seven simulators demonstrating various principles of space travel. The "multiaxis" is like a multidimensional lettuce dryer. The space wall, where you try to open doors and undo bolts while strapped into a chair that simulates weightlessness, is a refreshingly sedate experience in comparison.

By the way, the rocket ship out front is a three-quarter scale replica of the *Ariane IV*, the European satellite launcher that made its debut in 1988. The *Ariane* series has launched several Canadian satellites, including the *Anik E2* in 1991. At 46 m, the replica is as tall as a 15-storey building.

2150 Highway 15
(450) 978-3600

Season and Hours
10 a.m.–6 p.m. Tues–Sun, all year.

Fees
Adults $8.75, students $5.50, seniors $6.50, children 6 and up $5.50, family $23.

Directions
Take Highway 15 (Laurentian Autoroute) north to exit 9 (St Martin Blvd West). From there, follow the signs 3 km to the entrance. Bus: Orange line to Henri Bourassa, 60 bus to behind Travel Lodge hotel.

38

The
Armand Frappier
Museum

A n old two-storey brick house sits on the shores of the Rivière des Prairies in Laval. There are pretty flowers in hanging pots, and its wooden porch is neatly swept. Inside this humble building is a tiny museum dedicated to Armand Frappier, the doctor who, over a period of 30 years, developed six million tuberculosis vaccines and distributed them throughout Quebec.

TB is a gruesome and highly contagious disease that creates gnarled growths called tubercles in the bones, joints or lungs. It is now mercifully rare in the developed world (although there has been a recent resurgence), but tubercular lesions have been found on the bones of skeletons dating back 5,000 years.

Treatments before the age of antibiotics were varied and not very effective—bloodletting, bed rest and even the touch of a king or queen's hand. In 17th century Europe, one in four deaths was due to TB. Scientists were therefore keen on developing preventive measures.

With its strong focus on Dr Frappier and the disease he sought to eradicate, this museum will be greatly appreciated by those with a keen interest in medical research or biography. It puts science on a human scale, turning a 50-year battle to prevent TB in Canada into a personal story.

Frappier was born into a family of modest means in 1904, and his own mother died of TB when he was just 19. One of his professors at the University of Montreal, Dr Télésphore Parizeau (grandfather of the former premier of Quebec), obtained a scholarship for him to study in the United States. From there he went to Paris, where he learned the secrets of vaccination.

A vaccine is the "harmless" form of a bacillus that produces an immune response in a host without causing the disease. This enables the host to fight off exposures to the real disease. The first vaccine was for smallpox, which was extracted in its harmless form from animals and used successfully in people in the 1880s.

Tuberculosis was a tougher nut to crack. It took two French scientists, Calmette and Guérin, 13 years to transform the bovine tuberculosis bacillus into a form that could be used to vaccinate humans safely. They did so by nourishing it in Petri dishes, injecting cows with the new generations and observing the results. It was this vaccine that Frappier cultured and distributed in Canada.

The first floor of the house is an almost shrine-like homage to Frappier. One case displays his Order of Canada medal next to a garden trowel (Frappier was an avid gardener). Another contains notes from his home laboratory—by the way, a *"queue de rat"* is actually a rat-tail file!

The upstairs exhibits go into the long history of TB and explain the process of vaccine creation through displays of scientific equipment and large panels on the walls. While it is not exactly a hands-on museum, three microscopes are set up so you can see how advances in optics allowed scientists to finally view the tubercle bacillus.

Famous victims include composer Chopin, poet Keats, T. E. Lawrence (of Arabia) and half a dozen members of the famed English Brontë family. Among Canadian sufferers were Prime Minister Wilfred Laurier, who had the chronic non-fatal form and Dr Norman Bethune.

Despite vaccinations and modern treatments, the history of this disease isn't over yet. There are an estimated 30 million TB sufferers worldwide today and 8 million new cases each year. This little museum will be only too relevant for many years to come.

531 Des Prairies Blvd
(450) 686-5641
Tours available for groups of 10 or more with advance notice.
Season and Hours
Sept–June: Mon–Fri 9 a.m.–5 p.m.;
Jul–Aug: 10 a.m.–5 p.m. daily.
Fees
Adults $5, students and youth $2.50.
Directions
Orange line to Henri Bourassa, 20 or 20A bus to museum entrance, opposite the Armand Frappier Institute.

Old-Growth Forest
in the Boisé Papineau

S aved from development by an environmental group in 1986, the Boisé Papineau park is a very pleasant surprise in the heart of suburban Laval. These woodlands are not just rich in natural beauty, they contain some of the last old-growth forest on Île Jesus. Well-maintained packed-earth paths lead over the rolling terrain of a 15 ha maple and beech forest, beside marshlands and alongside a small pond or two. Two streams also traverse the park. Used mainly by school groups in spring and skiers in winter, the park's attractions are its wild terrain, minimal development and easy strolls.

A map available in the community centre at the park entrance is somewhat helpful, but doesn't show the true lay of the land nor reflect the trails perfectly. One of the park's nicest features, a large pond crowded with cattails, isn't shown on the map, but is certainly worth seeking out. Large flat-topped stepping stones have been laid out across the water, leading to a dead-end trail on the rugged, though small, sloping hill on the far shore.

Despite the misleading map and complete absence of signage in the park, it isn't difficult to find your way on the 3.5 km of trails. At one time, many trails crisscrossed the woods, but since park managers have closed quite a few of them in an effort to encourage regrowth, it's hard to get lost. Also, the park is bordered to the west by Highway 19, to the north by Highway 440 and to the east by hydro lines. It is bisected by a railway line.

A few hundred metres into the woods the main trail forks. The right branch leads to marshland by the train tracks, where it comes to a dead end at one of the streams. (There is no trail alongside the other stream, across the tracks.)

The left branch is more interesting. Not far along, the path widens at a T-junction. Towering over the clearing are two beech trees, well over 100 years old, scarred where people have carved their initials into the bark. (Beech tree wounds get bigger as the tree grows.) If you take the wide, sandy steps down the hill to the right, you will eventually meet up with the other branch of the path. To get to the pond with the stepping stones, continue along the main trail and take the first branch to the left. Don't bother taking the second left, since that leads to a housing development.

Most of the park is across a railway line from the main entrance. For the time being, getting to it requires trekking through wetlands and clambering up and over the train tracks, or walking through a stream and culvert. A bridge is planned, which is a good thing, since this section may turn out to be the most interesting part of the park.

Boisé Papineau is very popular in spring when trilliums bloom, covering the forest floor, and in autumn, when the maple and beech leaves change colour. In winter cross-country skiers make use of many additional trails, and a waxing room is set up in the community centre.

The only toilets are in the community centre, and there are no areas suitable for a picnic in the park itself, though there are half a dozen tables behind the community centre. Dogs are welcome, but must be kept on a leash. If you go in summer, take plenty of insect repellent, since the mosquitoes are fierce.

3235 St Martin East
Community centre: (450) 662-7610
Laval Recreation Department (Duvernay): (450) 662-4901
Season and Hours
Park: Sunrise–sunset.
Community centre: Mon–Fri 8 a.m.– 10:30 p.m., Sat 8 a.m.–5 p.m.
Fees
Free.
Directions
Orange line to Henri Bourassa. Take 31, 60 or 72 bus to St Martin Blvd and Des Laurentides Blvd. Transfer to 50 bus east to park entrance.

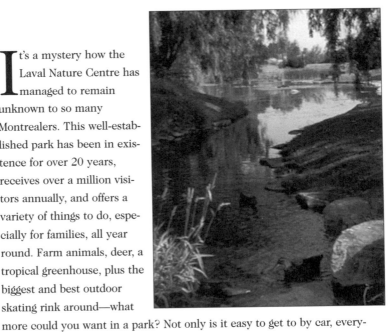

Four-Season, All-Weather
Fun at the Laval
Nature Centre

It's a mystery how the Laval Nature Centre has managed to remain unknown to so many Montrealers. This well-established park has been in existence for over 20 years, receives over a million visitors annually, and offers a variety of things to do, especially for families, all year round. Farm animals, deer, a tropical greenhouse, plus the biggest and best outdoor skating rink around—what more could you want in a park? Not only is it easy to get to by car, everything, including admission and parking, is free.

The nature centre is located in an old quarry on the south edge of Île Jésus, just west of the Pie IX Bridge. Though thoroughly landscaped, the quarry is still discernible in the cliffs that plunge straight into the large artificial lake that was once the main pit.

Children will enjoy a stroll through the small, modern, clean barn, just on the other side of the lake from the main entrance. It houses a number of animals, including a cow, a horse, some pheasants, a huge pig that tips the scales at over 300 kg—even a farm cat and a couple of mice. Part of the barn has been turned into an indoor duck pond, with a bridge over it for viewing.

Next door is a greenhouse full of tropical plants and exotic birds, both caged and flying loose. The Japanese carp in the fast-flowing pool are actually part of the school at the Botanical Garden. This is a co-operative safety precaution between the two installations; if the fish at one park die of disease, there will be others available for restocking. These beautiful creatures can cost upwards of several thousand dollars apiece—so no fishing!

Just up a hill from the barn and greenhouse is another surprise, a large chain-link enclosure with nine white-tailed deer.

All the facilities are open in winter, when the park turns into a hub of outdoor activity. To 3 km of cleared walking paths, the centre adds 7 km groomed for cross-country skiing and skate-skiing. There is a small hill with several slopes for tobogganing, too, but the *pièce de résistance* is the giant skating rink on the artificial lake. It covers an area about the size of 18 hockey rinks. Call ahead for ice conditions, since the lake is very deep and consequently the ice takes some time to freeze. The park management claims it's the best outdoor ice in Quebec, and there's little reason to doubt it: The lake is cleared and maintained using a Zamboni machine! (The Bonsecours Basin in Old Montreal is the only other outdoor rink to Zamboni its ice.)

You can rent skates, have yours sharpened, or just stop in for a snack and some hot chocolate in the lakeside chalet.

Both winter and summer, the centre provides an extraordinary amount of free family entertainment (in French only). On most weekends, and weekdays during school holidays, there are special activities ranging from treasure hunts to dogsledding. Over 70,000 people gathered in the park for family fun and an outdoor concert last St Jean Baptiste Day (June 24).

In summer you can rent canoes and kayaks for a paddle around the lake.

54 Parc
(450) 662-4942

Season and Hours
Chalet and other buildings:
9 a.m.–10 p.m.

Fees
Admission free. Parking (weekends and special events) $3. Canoe rental $3/25 min, kayaks $2/25 min.

Directions
Take Highway 15 (Laurentian Autoroute) north to Highway 440 (Laval Autoroute). Take the 440 east to Highway 19 (Papineau Autoroute), then follow Highway 19 south (towards Montreal) to exit 5 (Concorde Blvd). Follow Concorde Blvd east to Avenue du Parc. The park is bordered by Concorde Blvd to the south, St Martin Blvd to the north, and Highway 25 to the east. The main entrance is on Avenue du Parc.
Bus: Orange line to Henri Bourasaa, 54 bus to Parc.

North and East

⚜ White-tailed deer ... a popular fishing hole ... caverns clawed out of the earth 20,000 years ago by glaciers—not quite what you'd expect to find in a part of the city better known for the

Olympic Stadium and Botanical Garden. A mainly residential area with some industrial zones, the northeast end of Montreal is full of natural surprises, too. ⚜ In addition to a chance to go underground in the St Léonard caves, this section presents the island's last remaining marshland (and wild deer) in the Pointe des Prairies Nature Park, so named because it straddles the easternmost districts of Pointe aux Trembles and Rivière des Prairies. A little closer to centre is a trip to the old Miron Quarry, where a guided minibus tour takes you deep into the city's rapidly filling dump—an unlikely sounding day trip, perhaps, but quite fascinating. The nearby Île de la Visitation Nature Park is a semi-urban park in a historic district, with a lovely island you can walk around in about 20 minutes. ✺ For the city's best waterslides, head

to Rivière des Prairies Aquatic Centre. Tucked away on the edge of the back river, it has a great hot tub, too. The Botanical Garden and Insectarium are familiar attractions, but some of their activities are rather exotic and well worth investigating.

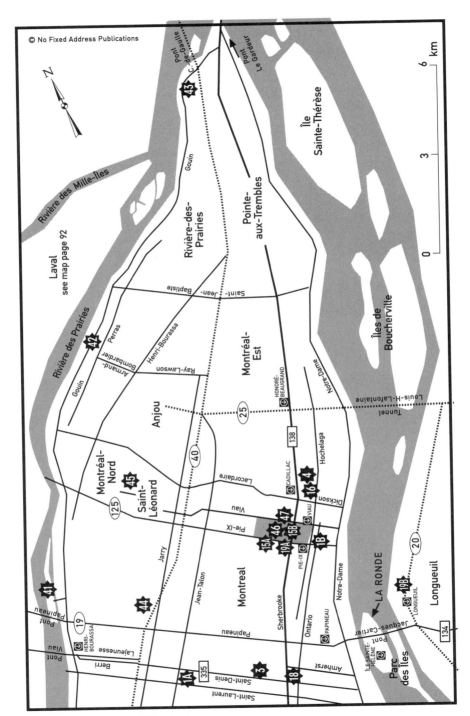

© No Fixed Address Publications

N

km

Laval
see map page 92

Rivière des Mille-Îles

Rivière des Prairies

Rivière-des-Prairies

Pointe-aux-Trembles

Île Sainte-Thérèse

Îles de Boucherville

Gouin

Perras

Bombardier

Armand-

Henri-Bourassa

Ray-Lawson

Saint-Jean-Baptiste

Anjou

Montréal-Nord

Saint-Léonard

Montréal-Est

HONORÉ-BEAUGRAND

Notre-Dame

Louis-H-Lafontaine

Tunnel

Lacordaire

Dickson

Hochelaga

CADILLAC

VIAU

Viau

Pie-IX

PIE-IX

Jarry

Jean-Talon

Montreal

Sherbrooke

Notre-Dame

LA RONDE

Longueuil

LONGUEUIL

Gouin

Pont Le Gardeur

Pont de Gaulle

C.

Papineau

Lajeunesse

HENRI-BOURASSA

Berri

Pont Viau

Pont Papineau

Saint-Laurent

Saint-Denis

Papineau

Ontario

Amherst

PAPINEAU

Pont Jacques-Cartier

ÎLE SAINTE-HÉLÈNE

Parc des Îles

25

40

125

138

19

335

134

20

TRIP DESTINATIONS
(denoted by star symbol on map)

41. Île de la Visitation Nature Park
2425 Gouin Blvd East
(514) 280-6733
p. 110

42. Rivière des Prairies Aquatic Centre
12515 Rodolphe Forget
(514) 872-9322
p. 112

43. Pointe aux Prairies Nature Park
12300 Gouin Blvd East
(514) 280-6688
12980 Gouin Blvd East
(514) 280-6772
14905 Sherbrooke St East
(514) 280-6691
p. 114

44. St Michel Environmental Centre (Miron Quarry)
2525 Jarry East
(514) 872-0761
p. 116

45. St Léonard Cavern
5200 Lavoisier (Pie XII Park)
Reservations: (514) 252-3323; Park
Office: (514) 252-3006
p. 118

15A, 15B, 46 & 47. Botanical Garden and Insectarium
4101 Sherbrooke East (Pie IX)
(514) 872-1400
p. 42, p. 120, p. 122

1A. Jean Talon Market
7075 Casgrain
(514) 277-1588
p. 12

1B. Maisonneuve Market
4445 Ontario East (Letourneux)
(514) 937-7754
p. 12

16. Centre d'Escalade Horizon Roc (Rock climbing)
2350 Dickson
(514) 899-5000
p. 44

18. Écomusée du Fier Monde
2050 Amherst
(514) 528-8444
p. 48

19A. Fédération Québécoise de la Marche (Quebec Walkers' Federation)
4545 Pierre de Coubertin
(514) 252-3157
p. 50

19B. JASS
Longueuil metro
(514) 338-8727
p. 50

TOURIST INFORMATION

MUC Nature Parks Info Line
(514) 280-PARC (7272)

Île de la Visitation
Nature Park

In 1928 Île de la Visitation was almost completely levelled to build the Rivière des Prairies hydro dam. Massive amounts of earth were shifted to turn the island into an active component of the project, resulting in three artificial basins, a spillway and a drop in water level of several metres between one side of the island and the other. In 1983 it was acquired by the Montreal Urban Community and turned into the first nature park. Thoroughly replanted, with new bushes and trees added each year, it has become a little island paradise in the 300-year-old district of Ahuntsic.

The mainland portion of the park is typical of many urban parks, pleasant, but mainly unspectacular. The eastern end is an exception, however. On the path nearest the water, there are several nice views of the island and a remarkable structure at its eastern limit: a concrete spillway 100-odd metres long, with water cascading over it. You can scramble down to walk along the rocky shore at a number of places.

The real prize is the island, a long sliver of land a few dozen metres off the mainland and running parallel to it. Just east of the visitor's centre, a metal and wood bridge spans the narrow basin near the end of the island. On the very tip of the island, a wooden gazebo overlooks the dam and spillway. In some places along the path, you can see both the river and the basin—the contrast in water levels is startling.

There is lots more happening at the western end, where the island is more wooded and quite a bit broader. Half a dozen lucky families live here, some in small farmhouses dating from the turn of the century. This is also where the best picnic sites are, one on a large grassy area around a gigantic old tree and another on the edge of a basin, opposite the houses. (Note that the only toilets are on the mainland in the visitor's centre.)

If you have time, it's worth continuing along the path and under the highway to the Bassin de l'Église (Church Basin). Here water rushes in via a large artificial inlet, then spills into the second basin before finally running under the ruins of an old millhouse and back into the river. The mad swirl of water must mean good fishing, since there are always people trying their luck. You might want to double back from here, since the paths along the basin's edges are rough, and following them onto the mainland means a boring walk through residential streets to return to the park.

A second bridge leads over the river beside the ruins of an old mill, where five sluices provide a great noise of rushing water. The recently restored millhouse is open for visits, and houses toilets, a boutique and riverside café.

Nearby, a children's exhibition (in French only) at the Maison du Pressoir presents the early history of the area, when Ahuntsic was a small village isolated from Montreal. A highlight is the full-sized cider press from which the house derives its name. You can purchase a booklet (also in French only) for a self-guided walking tour of 25 historic houses in the district. The Église de la Visitation is a good example of the architectural treasures in this area. Built in 1752, it is the oldest church in Montreal.

2425 Gouin Blvd East
(514) 280-6733

Season and Hours
Park: Sunrise to sunset, every day.
Visitor's Centre: Late April–Labour Day:
9:30 a.m.–6 p.m.; Labour Day–late Oct:
9:30 a.m.–4:30 p.m.; Mid-Dec–
mid-March: daylight hours.
Call (514) 280-PARC (7272) for most
recent hours.

Fees
Free.

Directions
Orange line to Henri Bourassa, 69 bus
east to De Lille Rd. Walk north on De
Lille to park entrance.

Splishin' and Splashin'
at the
Rivière des Prairies
Aquatic Centre

Nestled between a small public library and a college on the banks of the back river in northeastern Montreal, the Rivière des Prairies Aquatic Centre is a little tropical paradise. Sunlight streams in through a wall of windows. Lifeguards sit in the shade of an artificial palm tree on the tip of a small peninsula. Real trees grow in planters all around. The huge, high-ceilinged main room contains three gorgeous wading pools, a whirlpool bath and the best waterslides in town. Last one in is a rotten egg!

Like LaSalle's Aquadome (see page 14), the Aquatic Centre was built with families and teens in mind. It has family changing rooms and an eating area with vending machines, where brown-bag lunches are welcome. There are pool-side lounge chairs and tables, as well, and in warm weather the back door opens onto a spacious lawn and patio with room for about 50 people.

The design of each of the three extra-large wading pools is different. One has an inlet in the centre, where the water swells gently with the flow. Another has a mushroom-shaped fountain that comes in handy for tag, hide-and-seek or just getting a good dousing. The third pool has a gradually sloping "beach entry" for toddlers and wheelchairs and a tall water-spitting dragon fountain in the middle. The water temperature in the wading pools is a comfy 28.5°C, while the air temperature is a tropical 30°C—and even the bottoms of the pools are heated. A beautiful touch has the three pools at different levels, separated by planters, with water cascading between them.

But what really puts this centre into a league of its own are the two side-by-side water slides with their own pool. These giants are two stories high, rivalling the larger outdoor fun-park slides. They are monstrously fun, twisting and turning every which way before dumping you in a rush of water into the catch-basin. Monitors at the top ensure a safe departure, and there are lifeguards standing by at the bottom for those who need help getting out, as the current is rather strong. To use the slides you must be at least 112 cm tall and know how to swim.

For serious swimmers, the Aquatic Centre has a 50 m pool with lanes and two diving boards (1 m and 3 m). If you prefer to relax in the water, you can have a soak in the full-size hot whirlpool bath.

In addition to year-round family fun, the Aquatic Centre offers a number of courses for all ages, including aqua-fitness, prenatal fitness, life-guarding and all levels of swimming.

Bathing caps are not required at the centre, but you should bring your own lock for safeguarding your valuables.

12,515 Rodolphe Forget
(514) 872-9322

Season and Hours
Spring hours are given. Call for up-to-date information.
Family hours (wading pools):
Tue–Fri 11 a.m.–3 p.m. and 5 p.m.–7:30 p.m., Sat 9 a.m.–12 p.m.
Family hours (slides and fountains):
Tue–Fri 7:30 p.m.–8:30 p.m., Sat–Sun 12 p.m.–3:30 p.m..
For all (25 m pool):
Tue–Fri 3 p.m–5 p.m.
Adults only (all pools and slides):
Tue–Fri 8:30 p.m.–9:30 p.m., Sat 3:30 p.m.– 4:30 p.m..
Adults (wading pools):
Tue–Fri 10 a.m.–11a.m.

Fees
Free.

Directions
Orange line to Henri Bourassa, 49 bus (Léger) to corner of Rodolphe Forget.

Bikes, Birds and Wild Deer in
Pointe aux Prairies
Nature Park

Straddling the island's eastern-most districts of Rivière des Prairies and Pointe aux Trembles is a park full of surprises. Its northern end is a marshy area on the back river, teeming with waterfowl. The central wooded sector is ideal for cycling and walking (or skiing in winter). And in the park's unnamed and undeveloped southernmost reaches, about a dozen wild white-tailed deer roam its unfenced lands.

The Rivière des Prairies area is in many ways the loveliest part of the park. The only marshland on the island of Montreal is here, and there are several ponds where you'll see ducks, Great Blue Herons and Night Herons, among others. If you're on foot, you might like to proceed along one of the paths heading east from the marsh pavilion (the nicest of the two visitor's centres serving this area). These lead to a large pond with a healthy marsh-to-pond ecotone. A broad and sturdy wooden walkway with heavy rope rail-ings crosses the most open area. In the middle, a covered deck with a Polynesian air has benches where you can sit and observe several birdhouses out over the water.

Another way to get a good look at the park is from the visitor's centre stone observation tower that offers a 360-degree view. The centre is also the place to have a snack, get oriented or pick up a map of the park. (The trails are signposted, but you're better off carrying your own map.) The high-tech windmill beside the centre was intended to generate electricity to control

water levels in the pond and marsh, but it is broken, so for the time being water is being pumped using regular electricity.

A narrow strip of land connects the north edge of the park to the central Heritage Woods, winding by the MUC sewage-treatment plant and over Highway 40 on the edge of a carefully fenced railway bridge. On some days the odours emanating from the plant are rather unpleasant, but the park has done its best: In several areas sweet-smelling wild rosebushes have been planted alongside the path. Trees would make a nice addition, since this is a somewhat shadeless and exposed area.

The central region is also beautiful, with numerous paths (some for pedestrians only) crisscrossing an older mixed maple and beech forest. The paths are well maintained and quite narrow, for a very woodsy experience. This part is popular with local families, since there is a large picnic area beside the park's third visitor's centre. In winter, it becomes the focus for the network of cross-country ski trails—it is nearer the woods and has a large fireplace. There is also has a small hill for tobogganing.

The park continues south of Sherbrooke St, but the road is more like a wide and bumpy country lane, too straight and open to be very interesting. At any rate, it pales in comparison to the winding paths in the wooded areas. However, there are a dozen or so white-tailed deer living in this part. You'll spot them, if you're lucky, east of the path, along the railway line that cuts through this area. South of Notre Dame St, the park reaches the St Lawrence River, in an uninteresting open field by the ruins of an old house.

MARSH VISITOR'S CENTRE
12300 Gouin Blvd East
(514) 280-6688

RIVIÈRE DES PRAIRIES VISITOR'S CENTRE
12980 Gouin Blvd East
(514) 280-6772

HERITAGE WOODS VISITOR'S CENTRE
14905 Sherbrooke St East
(514) 280-6691

Season and Hours
Park: Sunrise to sunset. Visitor's centres: Late April–mid-October: 11 a.m.–5 p.m. Winter and weekday hours can vary. Please call.

Fees
Entrance free. Parking $4 (coins, Visa and Mastercard). Valid same day for all MUC nature parks.

Directions
Rivière des Prairies: Green line to Honoré Beaugrand. Take 189 bus to terminus, then 183 bus. Or, orange line to Henri Bourassa then 48 bus and 183 to the park.

Heritage Woods: Green line to Honoré Beaugrand. Take 189 bus west along Sherbrooke to Yves Thériault. Walk north to park entrance.

Down in the Dumps
at the
Miron Quarry

There is something very elemental about a visit to a dump. It might be the seagulls, or the huge machines roving end-lessly over piles of refuse, or maybe it's simply all that discarded history underfoot. Whatever it is, the City of Montreal's landfill site, the Miron Quarry, has it in spades. If you've ever wondered where all the stuff from those green and blue recycling bins goes, just take a guided tour of the dump and its recycling facilities.

An old lime quarry used as a dump since 1968, the Miron Quarry now goes by the name of the Complexe Environnemental de Saint-Michel (St Michel Environmental Complex), and for good reason. In addition to the massive landfill site, it contains a sorting and recycling centre, two compost-ing centres and a biogas centre.

What a strange feeling to travel roller-coaster roads winding through bleak lunar landscapes to rich mounds of compost, passing by specialized heaps simply overwhelming in their scale: concrete here, old furniture there. At 182 ha, the Miron Quarry is almost as large as Mount Royal Park, and at 70 m, it is nearly as deep as the mountain is high.

The sorting and recycling building receives all the contents of neighbourhood green bells and household green and blue boxes. (About 450,000 homes have curbside collection and more are added each year.) It is a large warehouse filled with huge bales of sorted material, where loose paper litters the floor. There are four conveyer belts, one each for paper, glass, plastic and metal. Men and women in blue jumpsuits, gloves and goggles sort and grade the material, tossing it down great funnels that lead to compactors.

On the way into the dump you'll get a drive-by tour of a large white building where electricity is produced using methane, or biogas, a natural product of decomposition. Throughout the site, 300 large pipes stick up from deep beneath the surface. These were originally installed to prevent danger-ous buildups of explosive biogas, and for years it was simply released into the air. In 1988 the wells were was capped and the gas was burned. Now the biogas is collected and used to generate 25 MW of electricity—enough to power about 10,000 homes.

Most impressive is the garbage dump itself. A steady stream of trucks deliver garbage day and night, half a million tonnes a year. This is the domain of two bulldozer-type machines: one that shifts the garbage and another that compacts it with huge spiked wheels.

Each fall, the City collects leaves bagged by residents. Here the bags are emptied by hand, loaded by huge forklift into a 35 t truck (one of the biggies you see in mines), then laid out in about a dozen rows 3 m high by 30 m long for composting.

There are a number of other interesting sights on the tour. One area is reserved for road-work refuse, which is reused in building new roads through the quarry. Yet another area is piled deep with bricks, re-bar and con-crete. There are also several large ponds where groundwater is collected and partial-ly purified using hydrogen peroxide. And one small area has been set aside to deter-mine the best kind soil for covering a sani-tary landfill, because after just 30 years in the service of the City, the quarry is almost full. It is slated to be turned into a park—but that's another story.

2525 Jarry East, St Michel
(514) 872-0761
Reservations required.
Season and Hours
Mon–Fri 9 a.m.–5 p.m.
Fees
Free.
Directions
Orange line to Jarry. 193 bus east to corner of Jarry and Iberville.

Caving
in St Léonard

A typical city park has grass and trees, and maybe a baseball diamond, soccer field or even a public swimming pool. In this sense, Pie XII Park (Pius the Twelfth) in central St Léonard is well equipped, but it has a little something extra, too. On the edge of a small forested area, a dozen wooden steps lead down to a metal-grille door set into a concrete wall. Behind the door and a heavy canvas sheet is a cavern. It is by no means large, but it is a natural formation, tens of thousands of years old, and a tour of it is a great introduction to the thrill of caving.

There are 500 or so caves in Quebec, of which about 50 are large enough to enter. There are actually three such caves in St Léonard, but *the* St Léonard cave, as it is called, is the only one open for visits. It has been a popular tourist attraction since 1811, when it was first mentioned in a newspaper. In 1978 the Quebec Speleological Society began offering tours to the general public.

Most caves are formed by the action of water on sedimentary rock. In a process that is painfully slow by human standards, the water washes away the limestone's water-soluble calcium carbonate bit by bit, creating galleries, stalactites, stalagmites and other formations. (In deserts grottoes can be formed by blowing sand.)

The cave in St Léonard was formed by the more recent and rarer action of glaciers. Some 20,000 years ago, when the whole area was under 3 km of ice, the advancing glacier tore open the ground and shifted slabs of rock over top. Additional work was done by water. The cave measures about 40 m long by 2.5 m wide and has a flat ceiling high enough to allow visitors to stand up comfortably.

To give you a taste for life underground, you'll be shown a brief slide show outlining how caves are formed and the various structures you can find inside. Next your guide dons a pair of caving coveralls, lights an acetelyne lamp and takes you down below.

Although all the stalactites—the stone "icicles" that hang down—have been broken off by a century's worth of visitors, there is still plenty to see. Your guide will point out ancient fossilized seashells, coral and a truly impressive sea-worm fossil about 10 cm long. These fossils were formed 350 million years ago, when Montreal was at the bottom of a great ocean. You can also see clearly where the rocks on opposite walls would fit back together. And if you look at the roof near the entrance, you can see where roots of trees have made their way into the cave.

Climbing around inside is actively encouraged. At the back end of the cave there are two ladders to get you down to the bottom, to 9 m below the surface. You'll need to squeeze a little to get to them, but there's no need to worry. Caves are incredibly stable structures, with changes occurring over millennia. About halfway to the back a small corridor splits off to the right.

You won't need any special equipment for your tour of the St Léonard cave, but warm clothes are a must, since the temperature inside is a crisp 6°C, with humidity close to 100%. You'll also want to wear old clothes, as climbing, crawling and squeezing through tight places can be a muddy business. You might also want to wear gardening gloves—the ladder rungs can be muddy, as well. A hard-hat and battery-powered headlamp are provided by the guide. Visits, including the slide show, last approximately 1.5–2 hours.

5200 Lavoisier
Info line and reservations:
(514) 252-3323
Office: (514) 252-3006
Reservations required. Maximum 16 people per visit. Minimum age 6.

Season and Hours
June–Aug: Tue, Thur, Fri, Sat 9 a.m., 10:50 a.m., 1:15 p.m., 3:05 p.m.; Wed 1:15 p.m., 3:05 p.m., 5:45 p.m. and 7:35 p.m. only.
Office hours: Mon–Fri 9 a.m.–5 p.m.

Fees
$6.50 per person.

Directions
Green line to Viau. 132 bus north on Viau to Lavoisier. Walk east on Lavoisier to the park.

46

A Trip to the Orient in the
Botanical Garden

Travelling abroad is always a thrill. You see wondrous sights, get a taste of how other people live, and return refreshed and invigorated. For my money, the Botanical Garden's Chinese and Japanese gardens are a quick trip onto foreign soil that is hard to beat. They are exotic, even romantic, but most of all, they are genuine. With a volunteer guide, you'll learn about the traditions and philosophies behind the gardens' ponds, brooks, fish, pagodas and pavilions. And the new shuttle service makes getting around a breeze.

In 1991, experts from Shanghai designed and built the **Chinese Garden**. Three hundred tons of decorative stones were imported from China for the rock gardens, ponds and pathways. Colourful pagodas were transported piece by piece from Shanghai. Everything was laid out according to Chinese traditions of aesthetics and spiritualism, carefully placed to generate the best *feng shui* (flow of spiritual energy). The result is an authentic Chinese garden, touted as the most significant outside China itself.

If the stones in the slate pathways seem a little oddly placed, it is intentional, designed to slow you down and put you in relaxed, contemplative mood. The Zen bridge that works its way across the pond at angles is another tradition. Its 90-degree turns prevent any evil spirits from following you.

Those with a keen eye might notice that the miniature trees and plants on display in one pagoda are different from the well-known bonsai type. In fact, bonsai come from Japan. In China, miniature potted landscapes are called *penjing*, the main difference being that the Chinese often put more than one plant or object per pot. Many of the *penjing* were donated in 1984 by China's foremost collector, Hong Kong's Wu Yee Sung. Some are hundreds

N O R T H   A N D   E A S T

of years old and worth a fortune.

Less vibrant than the Chinese Garden, perhaps, but ultimately more soothing, is the nearby **Japanese Garden**. Enter via the rose garden (10,000 bushes bloom from late June until Sept), or through a sweet-scented pine forest. This, too, is a traditional Asian garden, combining plants, water and rocks to create a sanctuary for the soul. Though it is the same size as the Chinese Garden, it appears much larger, probably because there is just one pavilion (a low structure), and Japanese gardens make extensive use of lawns.

The garden features a 9 m waterfall tumbling into a large serpentine pond, and the bonsai collection includes a rhododendron that looks like one big flower when it blooms (the leaves are small but blossoms are a normal size.) The garden's gingko trees are also very special. The fan-shaped leaves of this splendid tree have been found in fossils millions of years old. It is a very hardy tree, resistant to disease and pollution. There was a resurgence in its popularity when it was the first tree to grow after the atomic bomb was dropped on Hiroshima in 1945.

The Japanese Pavilion displays Japanese culture, furniture, clothing and art, presented with a rare finesse. Its courtyard reveals a Zen garden, in which pea gravel is carefully raked to resemble ripples in a pond.

A free shuttle train (wheelchair accessible) is a handy way to get around, with seven stops throughout the Botanical Garden. Before hopping on, pick up a map at the main greenhouse. Another useful pamphlet is "The Wonders of the Seasons," listing what's flowering, year-round. In winter the garden is open to cross-country skiing, and the main greenhouse, which has really been spruced up in recent years, makes another pleasant winter getaway.

4101 Sherbrooke East (Pie IX)
(514) 872-1400
Reservations required for tours in English or group tours.

Season and Hours

Gardens and greenhouses: 9 a.m.–5 p.m. daily (9 p.m. in summer). Shuttle bus: Every 20 min, 10 a.m.–5 p.m., May–Sept.
Office: Mon–Fri 8:30 a.m.–4:30 p.m.
Tours: Every day except Wed, 10:30 a.m. and 1:30 p.m.

Fees

Adults $9.50, youth 6–17 $4.75, seniors $7. Guide: $10 per guide (groups only).

Directions

Green line to Pie IX. Walk north on Pie IX (or take the 139 bus north one stop) to Sherbrooke, then walk east to entrance. Or, Green line to Viau, and free shuttle bus to Insectarium entrance, every 15 min.

Get Around Town! Montreal **121**

47

Eating Insects...
or Just Looking at Them
at the Insectarium

I n *Things Fall Apart*, a
famous novel by African
writer Chinua Achebe,
when the sky darkens as a
cloud of locusts fly overhead,
the people of the village run
outside and pray for them to
land. They do, and the vil-
lagers feast for weeks on the
giant grasshoppers. The people in Achebe's novel were not
starving, but like many around
the world, they considered
particular insects to be rare
delicacies.

In Zaire people enjoy the cricket season as much as we Quebeckers
delight in the summer's first strawberries. In Australia aborigines consider
the wiccheti grub—a thumb-sized white larva that lives under bark—an egg-
like treat, while the thorax of the more common sugar ant turns an ordinary
glass of water into a tangy delight.

The next time you're in Laos or Thailand enjoying the pungent gorgonzola
taste of *nam prik mangda* vegetables on rice, note that its main ingredient
is the ground-up giant water bug. Closer to home, in Mexico the same kind
of caterpillar that makes its way into some brands of tequila is roasted and
served in a spicy sauce on tortillas.

Here in Quebec we don't often think of eating insects, or even their by-products, with the exception of honey. But insects are high in protein and low in fat, making good nutritional sense. Each spring the Insectarium acts as cultural ambassador to this marginalized culinary world, serving up tasty dishes featuring insects front and centre (for aficionados) and as unrecognisable ingredients (for newcomers).

Under the guidance of Chef Jean-Louis Thémistocle, the students of the Institut de Tourisme et d'Hôtellerie du Québec (the Quebec Institute of Tourism and Hotel Management) prepare a variety of insect-based treats. Popular dishes that make their way onto the table each year are Mexican-style locusts, mealworm biscuits and pizza, and chocolate-covered crickets. Even the most squeamish will no doubt enjoy the creamy bee-larva chip dip, and children love the maple-syrup taffy on snow, complete with mealworms.

On average, the chef, sous-chefs and assistants serve up 150,000 bee larvae, 100,000 mealworms, 35,000 crickets and 10,000 migratory locusts—guess they landed in the wrong place!—at this event that attracts about 15,000 visitors annually.

Even if you don't hanker for insect snacks, you might enjoy a stroll through the Insectarium at another time of year. This small building on the edge of the Botanical Garden houses about 27,000 members of the insect kingdom. Most are carefully preserved behind glass, but there are living specimens as well, among them the giant Madagascar cockroaches 7 cm long, tarantulas, millipedes, assassin bugs and crickets. Look for the vented cages.

In summer, a butterfly house is set up on the grounds outside. You can walk through this giant net tent, surrounded by hundreds of butterflies native to Quebec, feeding on their favourite shrubs and trees. The newest annual event is the butterfly release, in which thousands of exotic butterflies are set free in the main greenhouse.

4101 Sherbrooke St East (Pie IX)
(514) 872-1400
Season and Hours
9 a.m.–5 p.m. daily;
June 18–Labour Day: 9 a.m.–7 p.m.
Insect tastings: Spring break (generally last week in Feb and first week in Mar) 1 p.m.–4 p.m.
Butterfly House: June 21–Labour Day.
Fees
Adults $9.50, youth 6–17 $4.75 seniors $7. Includes entry to the Botanical Garden.
Directions
Green line to Pie IX. Walk north on Pie IX (or 139 bus north one stop) to Sherbrooke, then walk east to entrance.

South Shore

❂ Traditionally, the South Shore extends from the town of Mercier in the west to Contrecoeur in the east, hugging the shores of the St Lawrence River and reaching 10 to 20 km inland. For the purposes of having fun, however, we've extended this region a dozen or so kilometres westward to include two riverside attractions: a terrific beach and an archaeologi-

cal dig. ❂ Just south of the island of Valleyfield is the town of St Timothée—a quiet place with a very lively waterfront. The Parc des Îles de St Timothée boasts one of the most pleasant beaches in the region of Montreal, and great trails for walking, biking and blading. ❂ Nearby in Melocheville, Pointe du Buisson is a working archaeological dig that welcomes visitors. Don't expect to see any Indiana Jones-type researchers deep in dusty trenches—it is a calm, low-key operation. But what you do get is 5,000 years of Native history, and a very attractive park on the edge of the river. ✿ For a taste of living history, drop by the South Shore Mohawk town of Kahnawake. Each year in early summer it hosts a competitive Indian powwow, attracting professional dancers from around the globe. ✿ The Canadian Railway Museum in St Constant presents the country's largest collection of rolling stock, and in a historic fieldstone house in the riverside town of St Lambert, the charming Marsil Museum offers insight into the social messages of clothing and textiles. ✿ A real diversity of destinations—and all of them easily accessible by bus.

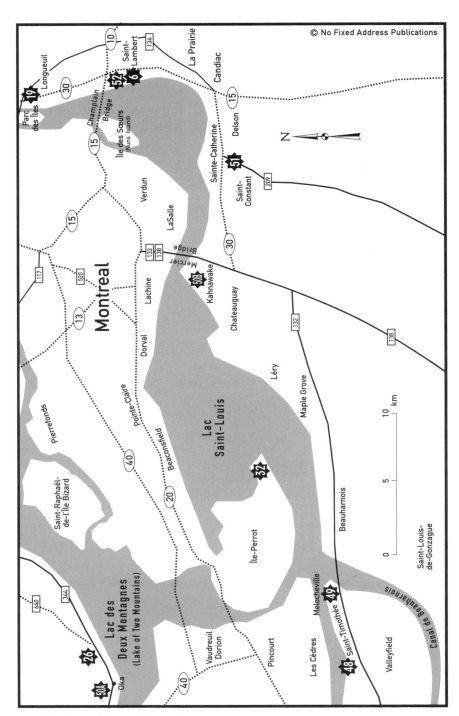

© No Fixed Address Publications

TRIP DESTINATIONS
(denoted by star symbol on map)

48. St Timothée Beach
240 St Laurent
St Timothée
(450) 377-1117
p. 128

**49. Pointe du Buisson
Archaeological Dig**
333 Émond
Melocheville
(450) 429-7857
p. 130

50A. Kanesatake Powwow
Kanesatake
(450) 479-8881
p. 132

50B. Kahnawake Powwow
Kahnawake
(450) 632-8667
p. 132

51. Canadian Railway Museum
122A St Pierre
St Constant
(450) 632-2410
p. 134

**52 & 6. Marsil Museum of Costume,
Textiles and Fibre**
379 Riverside
St Lambert
(450) 923-6601
p. 136, p. 22

19. JASS Hiking Club
Longueuil metro
(514) 338-8727
p. 50

TOURIST INFORMATION

Montérégie Tourist Association
(450) 469-0069

**Salaberry de Valleyfield and Suroît
Tourist Office**
(450) 377-7676, (800) 378-7648

48

St Timothée Beach

T

he St Lawrence Seaway is a series of canals, locks and dams designed to circumvent and pacify the many rapids between the Great Lakes and Montreal. The Beauharnois Canal, running south of the island of Valleyfield just west of Montreal, is one of its major constituents. As the canal neared completion in 1959, it became clear to the mayor of St Timothée that his town's waterfront was imperilled: Two separate canals and numerous dams in the region threatened to leave it high and dry.

Three hardworking mayors and 40 years later, the Parc Régional des Îles de Saint Timothée is a *fait accompli*. The series of islands that were once infamous markers of fierce rapids now sit in a calm backwater. The park offers a family-oriented beach and nature walks in a small, quiet, attractive setting with precious views of the islands.

Two short bridges—one for cars, the other for pedestrians—connect the town to Papineau Island, the park's main island. It is a pleasant five-minute walk along a shoreline path from the parking lot to the beach. If you have lots of gear, you might prefer to hop on the recently acquired Expo '67 shuttle train. Or, bring your bike or inline skates and cruise the 2 km asphalt path that loops around the park.

The beach is a small crescent of fine yellow sand that slopes gently to the crystal-clear waters of the basin. Three lifeguard towers keep an eye on the roped-off swimming area, where the water reaches a maximum depth of 1.70 m. The beach is backed by a large swath of grass laid out with picnic tables, a jungle-gym playground and two extra-large slides. Two regulation-sized beach-volleyball courts—i.e., set in sand—are available for pickup

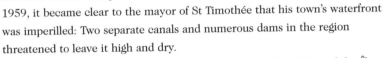

games. A deposit or ID is required to borrow a ball.

A very attractive visitor's centre with a large wooden deck overlooks the beach. It contains toilets and changing rooms, a snack bar with reasonable prices and a display on the history of the park. There are no security lockers for valuables.

In addition to the beach, the park has two conservation areas you can visit. One lies between the beach and the parking lot and is crisscrossed by narrow paths. The other is on a second island accessible via a gracefully arched footbridge. The smaller island has just one path, in the forest along the water's edge. Signs suggest staying on the path, but there isn't much temptation to do otherwise—the growth is wild and dense, and the trees are hung with vines.

From the tip of the island you have a good view of the St Timothée dam that controls the outflow from the basin. A dam across Juillet Island to the west controls the water flowing into it. The westward dam and numerous others aerate and purify the water to a quality normally found only in spring-fed lakes. The dams also put the beach at the mercy of Hydro-Quebec— at press time (summer '99), a strike had left it empty.

Special events include weekend kayaking lessons for groups of eight. In mid-July amateur astronomers gather for a telescope-building contest. In early August the water really churns as 200 scuba divers compete in a treasure hunt for $5,000 in prizes hidden in the basin.

Glass containers are not permitted on the beach, and food is allowed in the picnic areas only. Dogs are welcome, but not on the beach or in the playground areas. The beach, park and some paths are wheelchair accessible.

240 St Laurent, St Timothée
(450) 377-1117

Season and Hours

Mid-June–Labour Day 10 a.m.–5 p.m. weekdays, 10 a.m.–7 p.m. weekends. July 10 a.m.–7 p.m. every day.

Fees

Admission weekends: Adults $7, teenagers $5, children $3. Weekdays: Adults $5, teenagers $4, children $3. Single-seat kayak, two-seat pedalboat or canoe: $5/30 min, $9/hr. Two-seat kayak, three- or four-seat pedalboat $6/30 min, $11/hr. Single-seat pedalboat: $2/30 min, $4/hr. 16-seat *rabaska*: $18/30 min, $30/hr.

Directions

Car: Take the Mercier Bridge and Highway 132 west to St Timothée. In St Timothée, follow the signs, or turn south on St Laurent to the park entrance. Bus: Green line to Angrignon, then the Valleyfield bus (about 1 hr). For timetable and fares, see page 142.

49

Pointe du Buisson
Archaeological Dig
Melocheville

Photo: Pointe du Buisson Archaeological Park

F or 5,000 years before the arrival of Europeans, Pointe du Buisson (Scrub Point), a wooded peninsula jutting out into rapids on the St Lawrence just southwest of Montreal, was a summer campground for Native Canadians. The point was a natural resting place during the portage around the rapids, but it was the bounty of sturgeon that kept them coming back, summer after summer. The last tribes abandoned the area in the 15th century, leaving behind a wealth of information about themselves. Pointe du Buisson is now a working archaeological site with a visitor's centre and museum, plus wooded walks and a wonderful view of the St Lawrence.

The visitor's centre is a modern, ecologically designed building at the entrance. Since it also serves as the research centre, there isn't much on display here, though a model of the site and an ancient dugout canoe can provide some distraction for little ones while big ones sort through pamphlets and maps. A dozen tables on a wooden deck shaded by the forest are nice for a picnic, and food can be purchased in the snack bar.

On the tip of the peninsula, a short walk from the visitor's centre, is the museum, a small unpainted wooden structure built into a hillside. It presents the story of the people who lived here from 3000 BC to AD 1400. It has great

JULY/AUG

dioramas of fishing practices, showing both the activity above the water and the fish below. The Indians fished for sturgeon using hemp gillnets, by torch at night, or using a mesh wall and spears. And these were no little panfish. The largest sturgeon caught this century, for example, was 2.41 m long, and weighed in at 140 kg!

The Indians preserved their catch by smoking it, and on weekends in summer your admission ticket includes a taste of smoked sturgeon, store-bought, but heated over an open fire. (The construction of the Beauharnois hydro-electric dam brought an end to the fishing.)

Other exhibits include a terrific display of the awls, cutting edges and other implements used by Indians in daily activities, with an explanation of how the tools were made (pick up the English version by the door). Stone cutting edges were made using a technique called pressure-flaking. After the shape was roughly fashioned, an antler was used to apply great pressure to the edge. This delicate and time-consuming operation caused tiny chips to pop off the rock, resulting in an edge as sharp as that of a steel knife.

The archaeological excavation takes place on the wide lawn between the museum and the river. But you won't see any long dusty trenches or bucket bearers here. The wells are less than a metre square, and the bedrock is a mere 15–30 cm beneath the soil. Five thousand years of history in so little soil means the peninsula is extremely rich in artifacts—so far, over a million have been unearthed.

Two or three paths meander through the forest. The nicest one is the Chemin du Portage, with two wooden footbridges crossing over deep ravines. Be sure to bring insect repellent before venturing into the woods in summer!

There are two special weekends each summer, usually in late July and early August. On Indian Heritage Day you can feast on smoked sturgeon and roast corn, watch traditional dancing, listen to stories, light a fire using a flint or make a mask. On Archaeological Day you get to help out in the dig—and you're guaranteed to find an artifact.

(450) 429-7857

Season and Hours
10 a.m.–5 p.m. Mon–Fri, 10 a.m.–6 p.m. Sat–Sun, mid-May–Labour Day. 12 p.m.–5 p.m. Sat–Sun, Labour Day–Thanksgiving.

Fees
Adults $4, seniors $3, 6-17 $2.

Directions
Take the Mercier Bridge and follow Route 132 west. Bus: Green line to Angrignon, then the Valleyfield bus (about 45 min).
For timetable and fares, see page 142.

50

Indian Powwows
at Kahnawake and Kanesatake

Each year, on the weekend closest to July 11 (the anniversary of the Oka crisis), Montreal's Mohawk communities invite Natives and non-Natives alike to their powwows, traditional festivities of dance and music. For some of the finest dancing on the continent, visit the competitive powwow at Kahnawake. For a less crowded and more laid-back experience, drop by Kanesatake. Whichever you choose, you'll enjoy the friendly crowds, tasty food, and excellent dancing, drumming and singing.

Of the 500 or so Indian powwows in North America, the one on Tekakwitha Island in **Kahnawake** is the fastest growing. The stands are packed and there is standing room only when competitors from across the continent vie for over $30,000 in prize money.

Over the two days of the powwow, you'll see fancy dances, jingle dances, grass dances, and other traditional dances. Some of the men look truly fierce in their feathers and black makeup as they perform the sneak-up, commemorating the hunt. In the fancy dance, performers must know the steps and music intimately, timing the last step of their fast-paced dance with the last beat of the drum. Grass dancing enacts the stomping out of prairie grass fires. Each tribe has its own specialty, though some dances are shared by many tribes.

The costumes are marvellous. The women's are generally of a softer cut than the men's and are often decorated with up to 10 kg of beadwork and bells.

Starting Saturday at 9 a.m., you can take in the large arts and crafts sale or sample exotic foods such as buffalo burgers and Micmac salmon at over 50 food stalls. The Grand Entry at noon marks the beginning of the powwow. It is an impressive ceremony, led by elders carrying honour staffs decorated with medicines and feathers. The retiring of the flags closes the day at 7 p.m.

The **Kanesatake** powwow, held the same weekend, is more traditional. It has a very spiritual feel to it, with Indians coming from across Canada, the U.S., and as far away as Ecuador to dance for their Creator. You'll see a variety of excellent performances and have the chance to join in the fun during the intertribal dances. How often do you get to dance beside a fully costumed Mohawk warrior?

The chanting and drumming emanates from a central arbour, where musicians sit under the protective medicine of cedar branches. A master of ceremonies explains the significance of each dance. On the Friday before the weekend, a parade leads from the town of Oka, past the infamous pines, to the powwow grounds. Some years, early birds can join in the tobacco burning and prayer ceremony at sunrise.

There are some stands, but you might want to bring a blanket or lawn chairs and a picnic hamper. There are fewer food and crafts stalls at Kanesatake, but you'll still get a chance to sample Native fare, including a delicious corn soup. If you'd like to spend the weekend, you can bring a tent. Even if you don't stay over, take a stroll through the camping area for a great view from the little beach on the tip of the peninsula. (Swimming is not allowed.)

KAHNAWAKE

(450) 632-8667

Season and Hours

9 a.m.–7 p.m. (dancing from 1 p.m.) Sat–Sun, weekend nearest July 11.

Fees

General $8, youth 13–17 $4, elders and children 6–12 $3, children under 6 free.

Directions

Take the Mercier Bridge heading towards Route 138. Follow the signs for Kahnawake.

KANESATAKE

(450) 479-8881

Season and Hours

10 a.m.–late Sat–Sun, weekend nearest July 11.

Fees

General $6, elders and children under 12 free.

Directions

Take Highway 15 (Laurentian Autoroute) north to Highway 640. Follow the 640 west to the end and continue on Route 344 through Oka to Kanesatake. Bus: Orange line to Bonaventure, then CIT Rousillon bus to Kahnawake. For timetable and fares, see page 144.

51

Canadian
Railway Museum
St Constant

Take a trolley into the past, ride a diesel train or send a message by telegraph. Those are just some of the things you can do at the Canadian Railway Museum, where you could spend a good portion of the day inspecting the firsts, lasts, biggest and smallests of the engines and rolling stock that built and united our nation. The museum has examples of just about everything that ever set wheel to rail: locomotives, cabooses, passenger cars, trolleys—over 120 in all. The expansive grounds are anything but crowded, and since there are two large sheds, the railway museum is good fun even on a rainy day.

Youngsters will be thrilled and oldsters will feel nostalgic as they shake, rattle and roll on the streetcar that used to run along Ste Catherine Street. When the city took the last streetcars out of service, it hauled all 200 into a north-end field to be burned. At the last minute, this particular one was rescued, for sentimental reasons, because its number was 1959—the year of Montreal's last streetcar.

Another exhibit is the world's first pay-as-you-enter streetcar, which made its debut in Montreal in 1925. And then there's the school car, an invention that remained uniquely Canadian. From 1927 to 1967, specially built cars like this one served the railway towns of northern Ontario. The two cars of each teaching train contained a kitchen, living area and a classroom with 15 desks. (When a community had 16 school-age children, they could build a schoolhouse.) The cars stayed put for lessons, but moved from place to place on a weekly basis—kids were taught just one week of each month.

The *Dominion of Canada*, dating from 1937, is aerodynamic and brightly painted—unusual for a sooty steam engine. It was designed for speed and in 1939 it broke the world record for a train when it clocked over 200 km/h. That's Montreal to Toronto in two and a half hours! Kids will get a kick out of the "secret passage" alongside the boiler. Rumour has it that if you're quiet, you might hear the ghost that's said to live inside.

Another special sight is the *Golden Chariot*, an open-air streetcar with tiers of ornate seats, gilt ironwork and pastel yellow wood. In the days when seven tickets cost a quarter, the *Golden Chariot* offered a luxury tour of Montreal's Westmount and Mount Royal peaks for 50 cents.

An exhibit that is breathtaking in its proportions is the *Selkirk 5935*. It was built in 1949, when steam engines were rapidly being replaced by the cleaner diesel-electrics. The Canadian Pacific Railway wanted the biggest steam engine in the world. At 5 m tall, 10 m long and 365 t, they almost got it. The *Selkirk* is gargantuan.

Huffing and puffing demonstrations of the *John Molson*, a black, red and brass "choo-choo train"—a replica of an original built in 1849—are regularly scheduled on Sundays throughout the summer. The demonstrations are in the early afternoon, but the staff starts stoking the fire in the morning: It takes four hours to build the head of steam needed to put the engine into locomotion.

On Sundays you can also ride a diesel train or send a real telegram from Barrington Station, an authentic country station built in 1882.

122A St Pierre
(450) 632-2410

Season and Hours
9 a.m.–5 p.m., mid-May–Labour Day.

Fees
Adults $6, students $3.50, seniors $5, children 5–12 $3, children under 4 free. Cheaper during the week. Family rates available.

Directions
Go over the Mercier Bridge, take the La Prairie exit, then head east on Route 132. At the 5th traffic light, turn right onto Route 209 south. The museum is just before the train tracks, on the left-hand side. Bus: Orange line to Bonaventure, then CIT Rousillon bus 160 to museum.
For timetable and fares, see page 144.

52

Marsil Museum
of Costume, Textiles and Fibre
St Lambert

Photo: Pierre-Oner Castonguay

The Marsil Museum of Costume, Textiles and Fibre has a name that's nearly as big as the museum itself. This traditional fieldstone farmhouse is tiny by modern standards, with a single room on each of its two floors, but it makes a cosy museum. It is small enough that there's no risk of being overwhelmed by the number of displays, yet important enough that you'll see excellent exhibitions, carefully researched and elegantly presented. Depending on the current theme, you might get the chance to take a close-up look at costumes from famous theatrical productions or simply find out what's hip today. And there's always something for children to do on a Sunday afternoon.

The house, built in 1750, was one of the first in St Lambert. Its construction is typical of the period, with bell-cast eves extending over a front porch and dormers projecting from the roof. (Dormers were popular at the time—they turned a second floor into living space, although it was only taxed as an attic.)

The house has been renovated many times over the years, but its wide-plank wooden floors and exposed beams are original. And though the museum is a mere stone's throw from Highway 20, it has a warm, homey feeling you'd expect in a place tucked away in the countryside. Despite its smallness, earlier in this century four families lived there!

The Marsil Museum points out that clothing, as a universal part of the human experience, reflects not just personal taste, but political, economic, and cultural values as well. In "Common Threads: Cloth, Clothing and Culture," for example, one display showed how much a timeless Inuit *amauti* and a 1950s Christian Dior original have in common. Another illustrated the similarities between Ghandi's homespun cloth and the Quebec *étoffe du pays*, a hooded coat of grey homespun wool worn by *patriotes* of the rebellion of 1837.

Very rare and remarkable clothing and fabric are often on display. One exhibition featured a Victorian ball gown decorated with hundreds of pearls. But the museum is very much grounded in the community. During the "Cool Clothes" exhibition, grade-school students were asked to lend their favourite article of clothing and to tell the story behind it.

This is a small museum with a long reach. Most of the exhibitions are organized in conjunction with other institutions, which have included the Museum for Textiles (Toronto), the McCord Museum of Canadian History (Montreal) and the Canadian Museum of Civilization (Hull). The results are always enjoyable. Repeat visitors will note how remarkably the layout can change from one exhibition to the next.

The museum's reputation for excellence means that it can often catch travelling exhibitions as they make their way around the continent. In 1995, for example, the museum featured an exhibition of quilts, showcasing 20 of the country's top works, both traditional and modern. It was the first time the triennial event, sponsored by Rodman Hall (of St Catherines, Ontario) had found its way to a museum in Quebec.

The museum is set up for school groups, so there is always a hands-on activity for those who get fidgety. Children of all ages will enjoy the Sunday workshops (2 p.m.–4 p.m.). Keep an eye out for the special Christmas workshops held in early December.

379 Riverside
(450) 923-6601

Season and Hours
10 a.m.–4 p.m. Tues–Fri;
1 p.m.–4 p.m. Sat–Sun; all year.
Closed between exhibitions.

Fees
Adults $2, students and seniors $1, children under 12 free.

Directions
Take the Champlain Bridge (staying in the right-hand lane) and follow Highway 20 east towards Longueuil to exit 6. The museum is on the corner of Riverside and Notre Dame. Bus: Yellow line to Longueuil. Then 6, 13 or 15 bus along Riverside to Notre Dame.

Additional Destination Info

Art with Clean Hands at Paint-It-Yourself Ceramic Cafés (page 16)

CAFÉ ART FOLIE – NDG
5511 Monkland Ave, (514) 487-6066
Season and Hours: Mon–Thur
12 p.m.–11 p.m., Friday 11 a.m.–11 p.m.,
Sat 11 a.m.–12 p.m., Sun 11 a.m.–6 p.m.
Fees: Adults $8 for first hour, $4/hr afterwards; children under 12 and seniors $5 for first hour, $4/hr afterwards.
Directions: Orange line to Villa Maria. 162 bus to Girouard, or walk west along Monkland.

CAFÉ ART FOLIE – WEST ISLAND
3339C Sources Blvd (Centennial Plaza),
(514) 685-1980
Season and Hours: Tue–Fri 12 p.m.–10 p.m.,
Sat 10 a.m.–10 p.m., Sun 10 a.m.–6 p.m.
Fees: Adults $8 for first hour, $4/hr afterwards; children under 12 and seniors $5 for first hour, $4/hr afterwards.
Directions: Orange line to Côte Vertu. 215 bus to corner of Brunswick and Sources. Walk south through parking lot.

LA POTERIE
450B Beaconsfield Blvd (St Louis),
(514) 697-8187
Season and Hours: June–July: Mon
10 a.m.–4 p.m., Tue–Sat 10 a.m.–5 p.m.
Oct–Dec: Mon–Sun 10 a.m.–4 p.m.,
Tue–Wed 10 a.m.–6 p.m., Thur 10 a.m.–
9 p.m., Fri 10 a.m.–6 p.m., Sat 10 a.m.–
5 p.m., Sun 12 p.m.–5 p.m. Jan–May & Sept:
Mon 10 a.m.–4 p.m., Thur–Fri 10 a.m.–6 p.m.,
Sat 10 a.m.–5 p.m., Sun 12 p.m.–5 p.m.
Fees: Adults $7.50 for first hour, $4.50/hr afterwards; children $4.50/hr.
Directions: Orange or Green line to Lionel Groulx. 211 bus to St Louis Ave.

CERAMIC CAFÉ
4201B St Denis (Rachel), (514) 848-1119
Season and Hours: Mon–Wed
11 a.m.–11 p.m., Thur 11 a.m.–12 a.m.,
Fri 11 a.m.–1 a.m., Sat 10 a.m.–1 a.m.,
Sun 10 a.m.–10 p.m.
Fees: Adults $7 for first hour, $6/hr afterwards; children $5 for first hour, $4/hr afterwards.
Directions: Orange line to Mont Royal. Walk south on St Denis.

Indoor Karting (page 18)

F1 INDOOR KARTING
1755 Fortin, Laval (450) 629-2121
Season and Hours: 12 p.m.–11 p.m.
Sun–Thur, 12 p.m.–1 a.m. Fri–Sat.
Fees: Membership $5; race: $12 before
7 p.m., $15 after 7 p.m. Minimum age 16
(with parent first time) or 18.
Directions: Orange line to Henri-Bourassa,
60 bus along St Martin to Industrial (at underpass).

CIRCUIT 500
5592 Hochelaga, (514) 254-4244
Season and Hours: 24 hr, daily.
Fees: Membership $8; race: nonmembers
$16, members $12. Minimum age 14.
Directions: Green line to Assomption. Walk
south on Assomption, then east on Hochelaga
to Dickson, or 22 bus from the metro.

LES CIRCUITS IN-KART
7852 Champlain, LaSalle
(Place LaSalle mall) (514) 365-6665
Season and Hours: 12 p.m.–12 a.m.
Mon–Thur, 12 p.m.–1 a.m. Fri, 11 a.m.–1 a.m.
Sat, 11 a.m.–11 p.m. Sun.
Fees: Membership $8; race: $16 non-members, $13 members. Minimum age 16.
Directions: Green line to Angrignon, 110 bus to Place LaSalle.

Rainy Day Weekend Workshops for Children (page 22)

CANADIAN CENTRE FOR ARCHITECTURE
1920 Baile, (514) 939-7026
Reservations required.
Season and Hours: Sat–Sun, Nov–Apr, in conjunction with some exhibitions. Times vary.
Fees: Adults $4, children $2. May vary depending on exhibition.
Directions: Green line to Atwater, 15 bus along Ste Catherine to Fort or St Marc. Walk south to museum. Or, Green line to Guy-Concordia, 150 bus along René Lévesque to Fort or St Marc. Walk north to museum.

MONTREAL MUSEUM OF FINE ARTS
1379 Sherbrooke West,
(514) 285-1600 ext. 135 or 136
First come, first served.
Season and Hours: Sundays 12:30 p.m.–4:30 p.m., in 45 min sessions.
Fees: Free.
Directions: Green line to Guy-Concordia. Walk north to Sherbrooke, then east to museum. Workshops are on 1st floor, new building; ask at security.

REDPATH MUSEUM
859 Sherbrooke West (514) 398-4086, ext. 4092
Reservations required (leave message 9 a.m.–5 p.m.)
Season and Hours: Late Sept–mid-May: Sun 2 p.m.–3 p.m. (ages 4–7) and 3:30 p.m.–4:30 p.m. (ages 8–12).
Fees: Children $5.
Directions: Green line to McGill (McGill College exit). North on McGill College onto the campus. First left fork, building on the right.

MUSÉE D'ART CONTEMPORAIN
185 Ste Catherine West, (514) 847-6253
Season and Hours: Sun hourly 1 p.m.–4 p.m.
Fees: Adults $6, children 12 and up $3, under 12 free.
Directions: Green line to Place des Arts (Place des Arts exit). Corridor to the museum.

MARSIL MUSEUM OF COSTUME, TEXTILES AND FIBRE
379 Riverside, St Lambert, (450) 923-6601
Season and Hours: Sun 2 p.m.–4 p.m. during most exhibitions.
Fees: Adults $2, children $1.
Directions: Yellow line to Longueuil. 6, 13 or 15 bus along Riverside to Notre Dame.

Getting Hooked ... on Indoor Climbing Gyms (page 44)

ALLEZ-UP
1339 Shearer (SE corner at St Patrick), (514) 989-9656
Season and Hours: Mon–Tue 4 p.m.–11 p.m., Wed 2 p.m.–11 p.m., Thur–Fri 12 p.m.–11 p.m., Sat–Sun 9 a.m.–9 p.m.
Fees: Intro (1.5–2 hr) $35; accreditation only $5; single visit $11.25; equipment $7.50. Mon night women climb free; Fri two for one.
Directions: Green line to Charlevoix. Walk south on Charlevoix, then east on St Patrick to Shearer.

COLLÈGE ANDRÉ LAURENDEAU
1111 Lapierre St (corner La Verendrye), (514) 364-3320, ext. 249
Season and Hours: Mon–Fri 5:30 p.m.–10:30 p.m., Sat–Sun 10 a.m.–6 p.m.
Fees: Intro (3 hr) $40, accreditation only $15, single visit $10, equipment $1.50/part.
Directions: Green line to Angrignon, 113 bus to Lapierre. Walk north on Lapierre.

UNIVERSITÉ DE MONTRÉAL CEPSUM
2100 Édouard Montpetit (SW corner at Vincent d'Indy), (514) 343-6150, (514) 343-6993

Season and Hours: Mon–Fri 6:15 a.m.–
11:30 p.m., Sat–Sun 8:30 a.m.–11 p.m.
Reduced hours in summer.
iFees: Introductory course (8 hr over 2 days)
$125, accreditation only $19, single visit $9,
equipment $4.50.
Directions: Blue line to Édouard Montpetit.
Walkway to CEPSUM.

ACTION DIRECTE
4377 St Elzéar West (Curé Labelle),
(450) 688-0515
Season and Hours: Mon–Fri 9 a.m.–11 p.m.,
Sat 9 a.m.–10 p.m., Sun 9 a.m.–9 p.m.
Fees: Intro (2 hr) $35, accreditation only $4,
single visit $9.50, equipment $5.
Directions: Orange line to Henri Bourassa. 55
or 57 bus to St Elzéar and Curé Labelle. Or,
Orange line to Côte Vertu. 151 bus to St Elzéar
and Curé Labelle.

CENTRE D'ESCALADE
HORIZON ROC
2350 Dickson (SW corner at Hochelaga),
(514) 899-5000
Reservations required.
Season and Hours: Mon–Fri 10 a.m.–3 p.m.
(groups only), and 5:30 p.m.–11 p.m., Sat
10 a.m.–6 p.m., Sun 10 a.m.–5 p.m.
Fees: Introductory course (3 hr) $40, accredi-
tation only $9, membership $25/year, single
visit $11, equipment $8.50.
Directions: Green line to Joliette. Take 85
bus from metro to Dickson and Hochelaga.

The Best Views in Old
Montreal (page 56)

NOTRE DAME DE BON SECOURS
CHAPEL
450 Saint Paul East, (514) 282-8670
Season and Hours: Chapel: 10 a.m.–5 p.m.
Tue–Sun, only Sun when museum is closed.
Museum: May–Oct 10 a.m.–5 p.m. Tue–Sun;
mid-March–April & Nov–mid-Jan 11 a.m.–
3:30 p.m.; closed mid-Jan–mid-March.

Archaeological site (advance reservations
required): Thur–Sun 2 p.m. (English tour),
3 p.m. (French). Max. 7 per group.
Fees: Chapel: Free. Museum and tower: Adults
$5, seniors and students $3, 6–12 $2.
Archaeological site: $8 (includes museum).
Directions: Orange line to Champs de Mars
(St Antoine south exit). Walk south on Gosford
to St Paul, then east on St Paul to chapel.

CLOCK TOWER
QUAI DE L'HORLOGE
(Clock Tower Pier)
(foot of Place Jacques Cartier)
(514) 496-PORT (7678)
Season and Hours: May 1–mid-May
10 a.m.–7 p.m. Sat–Sun; mid-May–Labour Day
10 a.m.–9 p.m. every day.
Fees: Free.
Directions: Orange line to Champ de Mars (St
Antoine south exit). Walk south on Gosford to
St Paul, east to Bonsecours, then south.

CROISIÈRES AML (FERRIES)
Jacques Cartier Pier
(foot of St Lawrence), (514) 281-8000
Season and Hours: Longueuil Last weekend
May–June 24 & Labour Day–mid-Oct:
10:35 a.m.–7:35 p.m. Sat–Sun.
June 24–Labour Day: 10:35 a.m.–6:35 p.m.
Mon–Thur, 9:35 a.m.– 10:35 p.m. Fri–Sun.
St Helen's Island Last weekend May–June 24
& Labour Day–mid-Oct: 10:35 a.m.–7:10 p.m.
Sat–Sun. June 24–Labour Day: 10:35 a.m.–
7:10 p.m. Mon–Thur, 9:35 a.m.– 11:10 p.m.
Fri–Sun. Both ferries leave once an hour.
Fees: Longueuil $3.50. St Helen's Island: $3.
Both ferries: 8 tickets $20, under 6 free (one
child per adult), bicycles ride free. All tickets
one-way.
Directions: Orange line to Champ de Mars
(St Antoine south exit). Walk south on Gosford,
then west on Notre Dame to Place Jacques
Cartier and straight through square to the
Jacques Cartier Pier.

Keeping Kids Happy In Old Montreal (page 64)

Vieux Port de Montréal: (514) 496-PORT.
MayaVentura: (514) 869-9919.
IMAX: (514) 496-IMAX (4629).
Quadricycles: (514) 849-9953.
Pedalboats: (514) 282-0586.
Velo Aventure: (514) 847-0666
La Cerf-Volanterie: (514) 845-7613.
Season and Hours: Concession hours are longer in summer and vary with the weather. MayaVentura 10 a.m.–11:30 p.m. June 19– Labour Day. IMAX Year round. Call for schedule. Quadricycles May–Nov, weekends only after Labour Day. Pedalboats 12 p.m.–9 p.m. (11:30 p.m. on weekends) June–Labour Day. Weekends only May and Sept. Velo Aventure 9 a.m.–9 p.m. April 1–Oct 31. Kite demonstrations 1 p.m.–4 p.m. weekends.
Fees: MayaVentura: Adults $11.95, 13–17 $9.95, $4–12 $7.95, seniors $7.95. Family rates available. IMAX: Adults $12.50, seniors $10.50 13–17 $10.50, 4–12 $8.50, family (2 adults 2 children or 1 adult 3 children) $37.75. Quadricycles: Adults $5, 6–12 $4.20 per 30 min. Pedalocation du Vieux Port (pedalboats): Adults $5, 6–12 $4 per 30 min. Family (2 adults 2 children) $15. Velo Aventure Inline Skates: $9 first hr, $4.50 each additional hr, all protective equipment included. Bicycles: $7/hr, $22/day. Cheaper weekdays.
Directions: Orange line to Champ de Mars (St Antoine south exit). Walk south on Gosford into Old Montreal, turning left on Notre Dame to Place Jacques Cartier. Or, Orange line to Place d'Armes (St Urbain exit). Go south on St Urbain (becomes St Sulpice) to de la Commune.

Cap St Jacques Nature Park (page 74)

20099 Gouin Blvd West (Pierrefonds)
Visitor's centre: (514) 280-6871
Eco-Farm: (514) 280-6743
Château Gohier (near beach): (514) 620-4025
MUC Nature Parks Info Line: (514) 280-PARC (7272)
Season and Hours: Visitor's center May 1–mid-June & Sept 1–Oct 31: 10 a.m.– 5 p.m.; mid-June–end Aug 10 a.m.–7 p.m. mid–Dec–mid-March: 9:30 a.m.–5 p.m. Eco-Farm May 1–June 24 & Labour Day–Oct 31: 8:30 a.m.–4:30 p.m. June 24–Sept 6: weekdays 8:30 a.m.–4:30 p.m., weekends 8:30 a.m.–6 p.m. Winter: 9 a.m.–5 p.m. Château Gohier mid-June–last weekend Aug: weekdays 11 a.m.–4 p.m., weekends 11 a.m.–5 p.m. Mid-Dec–mid-March: weekdays 11 a.m.–5 p.m., weekends 10 a.m.– 5 p.m. Beach mid-June–last weekend in Aug: 10 a.m.–7 p.m.
Fees: Parking: $4 per day (valid for all parks). Canoe, kayak, pedalboat rental (mid-June– Sept): $8/hr. Beach: Adults $4, children 6-13 $3, seniors (60+) $3. Half price after 5 p.m.
Directions: Take Highway 40 west to exit 49 (Ste Marie Rd). Follow Ste Marie Rd west, then turn north on l'Anse à l'Orme Rd, and keep on it to Gouin Blvd. Head east on Gouin to the entrance. Bus: Orange line to Côte Vertu. Take 64 bus to Cartierville terminus, then 68 bus to park entrance.

Bois de Liesse Nature Park (page 86)

9432 Gouin Blvd West
Pitfield House (bike rental): (514) 280-6729.
Fields area visitor's centre: (514) 280-6678.
Peninsula area discovery centre:
(514) 280-6829.
MUC Nature Parks Info Line:
(514) 280-PARC (7272).
Season and Hours: Park: All year, sunrise–sunset. Pitfield House: May 1–Oct 31: 11 a.m.–4 p.m. Mon–Thur, 10 a.m.–5 p.m. Fri–Sun; mid-Dec–mid-Mar: weekdays 10:30 a.m.–4:30 p.m., weekends 9:30 a.m.–4:30 p.m. Fields area visitor's centre May 1–May 30 & Aug 30–Oct 31: 10:30 a.m.–5:30 p.m.; May 31–Aug 29: 11:30 a.m.–6:30 p.m. Winter hours subject to weather conditions.
Fees: Parking $4 per day (valid for all parks). Bike rental (May–Oct) $4–$6/hr, $6–$9/2 hr, depending on model.
Directions: Take Highway 20 or 40 west to Highway 13. Follow Highway 13 north to exit 8 (Gouin Blvd). Pitfield House: Turn left on Gouin. Entrance is 100 m along on left. Peninsula: Turn right on Gouin. Turn left immediately into park. Fields: Turn left on Gouin. Turn left immediately onto Pitfield. Turn right on Cypihot, then right on Douglas B. Floreani to park entrance.
Bus to Pitfield House: Orange line to Côte Vertu. 64 bus to Cartierville terminal (Gouin & Grenet), then 68 bus west to entrance. Or, Orange line to Henri Bourassa, 69 bus west to Cartierville terminal, then 68 bus. Bus to Fields area: Orange line to Henri Bourassa, 164 bus west to the corner of Henri Bourassa and Marcel Laurin. Transfer to 215 west on Henri Bourassa to Douglas B. Floreani. Walk north on Floreani to entrance.

SOUTH SHORE BUS SCHEDULES

St Timothée Beach (page 128)

Pointe du Buisson Archaeological Dig (page 130)

Bus service to St Timothée beach and Pointe du Buisson Archaeological Dig (Melocheville) is provided by CITSO (Commission Intermunicipal de Transport du Sudouest. Buses depart from the Angrignon metro station (Green line). Tickets are available at the Angrignon metro and at convenience stores in the destination towns. Exact fare required when paying on bus. CITSO ID card required for student and senior discounts.

Information: CITSO (514) 698-3030.
Office hours: Mon–Thur
8:30 a.m.–12:00 p.m., 1:15 p.m.–5:00 p.m.;
Fri 8:30 a.m.–12 p.m.

Fares: Melocheville: Adults $5.10, students $3.85, seniors $2.55, under 5 free with adult. St Timothée: Adults $5.70, students $4.30, seniors $2.85, under 5 free with adult.

Mon–Fri Schedule

Angrignon Metro	Melocheville	St Timothée	St Timothée	Melocheville	Angrignon Metro
06:30	07:17	07:28	05:22	05:33	06:21
07:45	08:32	08:42	06:32	06:43	07:31
08:15	09:02	09:13	07:02	07:13	08:01
09:50	10:35	10:46	08:27	08:36	09:42
11:10	11:55	12:06	10:02	10:12	10:59
12:40	13:25	13:36	11:37	11:47	12:34
14:20	15:05	15:16	12:57	13:07	13:54
15:50	16:37	16:48	14:37	14:47	15:34
16:40	17:27	17:38	16:07	16:17	17:04
17:20	19:07	18:18	16:42	16:53	17:39
17:50	18:37	18:48	17:37	17:48	18:36
18:45	19:30	19:41	18:42	18:53	19:37
19:50	20:35	20:46	20:32	20:42	21:29
21:55	22:40	22:51	22:32	22:42	23:29
23:40	00:25	00:36	23:38*	23:44*	00:29*
01:30*	02:15*	02:24*			
*Fri only.					

Sat–Sun Schedule
On weekends, the bus stops directly in front of the Pointe du Buisson Archeological Dig.

Angrignon Metro	Pointe du Buisson	St Timothée	St Timothée	Pointe du Buisson	Angrignon Metro
07:00	07:44	07:51	07:22	07:29	08:13
08:30	09:17	09:24	08:52	08:59	09:47
10:00	10:47	10:54	10:22	10:29	11:17
11:30	12:17	12:24	11:52	11:59	12:47
13:00	13:47	13:54	13:22	13:29	14:17
14:30	15:17	15:24	14:52	14:59	15:47
16:00	16:47	16:54	16:22	16:29	17:17
17:30	18:17	18:24	17:52	17:59	18:47
19:00	19:47	19:54	19:22	19:29	20:17
20:30	21:14	21:21	20:52	20:59	21:44
22:00	22:44	22:51	22:22	22:29	23:14
23:30	00:14	00:21	23:37	23:44	00:29
01:50*	02:34*	02:41*			
*Sat only.					

Kahnawake Powwow

(page 132)

There is a CITSO shuttle bus from the Angrignon metro station (Green line) on the weekend of the powwow. See above for office hours. Call for schedule.

Fares: Adult $3.30, 18–24 (with CITSO ID) $2.50, 14–17 (with CITSO ID), 6–13 $1.65, under 6 free.

The Canadian Railway Museum (page 134)

Bus service to the Canadian Railway Museum (St Constant) is provided by CIT (Conseil Intermunicipal de Transport) Rousillon. Buses depart from the Bonaventure metro station (Orange line), 1000 de la Gauchetière, south platform, door 16. Tickets are available on the bus.

Information (CIT Rousillon): (450) 638-2031 Office hours: Mon–Thur 9 a.m.–12 p.m. & 1 p.m.–16:30; Fri 9 a.m.–12 p.m. & 1 p.m.–3:30 p.m.

Fares: Adults $4.50, students and seniors $3 (with CIT Rousillon ID card), under 12 free when accompanied by an adult.

Bus	Place Bonaventure	Direction	Museum
Mon–Fri, June 21–Aug 13 (1999)			
160	9:10 a.m.	→	9:50 a.m.
160	12:10 p.m.	←	11:35 a.m.
160	4:45 p.m.	←	4:05 p.m.
Sat-Sun & legal holidays, June 19–mid-Oct 16 (1999)			
160	9:00 a.m.	→	9:40 a.m.
160	5:20 p.m.	←	4:40 p.m.

Quick Guide to Major Attractions

Museums and the Arts

Canadian Centre for Architecture
1920 Baile
(514) 939-7000
Metro: Guy-Concordia or
Georges Vanier

Canadian Railway Museum
122A St Pierre
St Constant/Delson
(450) 638-1522

Centre d'histoire de Montréal
335 Place d'Youville
(514) 872-3207
Metro: Place Victoria

Château Ramezay Museum
280 Notre Dame East
(514) 861-3708
Metro: Champ de Mars

Cosmodome
2150 Laurentian Autoroute
Laval
(450) 978-3600

Écomusée du Fier Monde
2050 Amherst
(514) 528-8444
Metro: Sherbrooke

Fleming Mill
9675 LaSalle
LaSalle
(514) 367-6486
Metro: Angrignon

Fur Trade in Lachine
1255 St Joseph
Lachine
(514) 637-7433
Metro: Angrignon – Bus 195

Leonard and Bina Ellen Art Gallery
Concordia University
1400 de Maisonneuve West
(514) 848-4750
Metro: Guy-Concordia

Maison Saint-Gabriel
2146 Place Dublin
(514) 935-8136

McCord Museum of Canadian History
690 Sherbrooke West
(514) 398-7100
Metro: McGill

Montreal Museum of Decorative Arts
2200 Crescent
(514) 284-1252
Metro: Guy-Concordia

Montreal Museum of Fine Arts
1379-80 Sherbrooke West
(514) 285-1600
Metro: Guy-Concordia/Peel

Musée d'Art Contemporain de Montréal (Modern Art)
185 Ste Catherine West
(514) 847-6226
Metro: Place des Arts

Musée d'Art de Saint Laurent
615 St Croix
Saint Laurent
(514) 747-7367

Musée des Hospitalières de l'Hôtel-Dieu de Montréal
201 Pine West
(514) 849-2919
Metro: Sherbrooke – bus 144

Musée Marc-Aurèle Fortin
118 St Pierre
(514) 845-6108
Metro: Square Victoria

Montreal Holocaust Memorial Centre
5151 Côte Ste Catherine
(514) 345-2605
Metro: Côte Ste Catherine

Pointe à Callière
Montreal Museum of Archaeology and History
350 Place Royale
(514) 872-9150
Metro: Place d'Armes

Place des Arts
260 de Maisonneuve East
(514) 285-4270
Metro: Place des Arts

Redpath Museum
859 Sherbrooke West
(514) 398-4086
Metro: McGill

Sir George-Étienne Cartier National Historic Site
458 Notre Dame East
(514) 283-2283
Metro: Champ de Mars

Stewart Museum at the Fort
St Helen's Island
(514) 861-6701
Metro: Île Nôtre-Dame
Selected Churches

Selected Churches

Christ Church Cathedral
535 Ste Catherine West
(514) 288-6421
Metro: McGill

Mary Queen of the World Cathedral
René Lévesque West
(at Mansfield)
(514) 866-1661
Metro: Bonaventure

Notre Dame Basilica
110 Notre Dame
(514) 842-2925
Metro: Place d'Armes

Notre Dame de Bon Secours Chapel (The "Sailors' Church")
400 Saint Paul St East
(514) 282-8670
Metro: Place d'Armes

St Joseph's Oratory
3800 Queen Mary
(514) 733-8211
Metro: Côte des Neiges

Selected Tourist Attractions

Infotourist Centre
1001 Dorchester Square
(south of Ste Catherine on Metcalfe)
(514) 873-2015
Metro: Peel

Old Montreal Tourist Bureau
174 Notre Dame East (NW corner Jacques Cartier Square)

Old Port of Montreal
Jacques Cartier Pier
(514) 283-5256 or
496-PORT (7678)

Biodome
4777 Pierre de Coubertin West
(514) 868-3000
Metro: Viau

Biosphere
160 Tour de l'Île
St Helen's Island
(514) 283-5000
Metro: Île Sainte Hélène

Descente sur le Saint-Laurent
(tours of Lachine Rapids)
LaSalle
(514) 767-2230;
(800) 324-RAFT (7238)

Imax Theatre
St Lawrence Blvd and de la Commune
(514) 496-IMAX (4629)
Metro: Place d'Armes

Lachine Rapids Jetboating and Rafting Tours
105 de la Commune West
(514) 284-9607
Metro: Champ de Mars

La Ronde
Parc des Îles de Montréal
(514) 872-4537
Metro: Île Sainte Hélène

Montreal Botanical Garden
4101 Sherbrooke East
(514) 872-1400
Metro: Viau

Montreal Insectarium
4101 Sherbrooke East
(514) 872-1400
Metro: Viau

Montreal Olympic Park
4141 Pierre de Coubertin
(514) 252-8687
Metro: Viau

Montreal Planetarium
1000 St Jacques
(514) 872-4530
Metro: Bonaventure (de la Cathédrale exit)

Molson Centre
1260 de la Gauchetière West
(514) 989-2873,
(514) 285-4270
Metro: Bonaventure or Lucien l'Allier

Hotels, Inns, Bed & Breakfasts

CENTRAL HOTELS

The Queen Elizabeth
900, boul. René-Lévesque
Ouest
Montréal (Québec) H3B 4A5
Metro: Bonaventure
Tel: (514) 861-3511
Fax: (514) 954-2258
Toll free: 1 800 441-1414

Le Centre Sheraton
1201, boul. René-Lévesque
Ouest
Montréal (Québec) H3B 2L7
Metro: Bonaventure/Peel
Tel: (514) 878-2000
Fax: (514) 878-2305
Toll free: 1 800 325-3535

**Montréal Marriott Château
Champlain**
1, Place du Canada
Montréal (Québec) H3B 4C9
Metro: Bonaventure
Tel: (514) 878-9000
Fax: (514) 878-6777
Toll free: 1 800 228-9290

Hôtel Wyndham Montréal
1255, rue Jeanne-Mance,
C.P. 130
Montréal (Québec) H5B 1E5
Metro: Place-des-Arts
Tel: (514) 285-1450
Fax: (514) 285-1243
Toll free: 1 800 361-8234
(Canada, U.S.)

**Radisson Hôtel des
Gouverneurs**
777, rue University
Montréal (Québec) H3C 3Z7
Metro: Square-Victoria
Tel: (514) 879-1370
Fax: (514) 879-1761
Toll free: 1 800 333-3333

**Holiday Inn Montréal-
Midtown**
420, rue Sherbrooke Ouest
Montréal (Québec) H3A 1B4
Metro: Place-des-Arts
Tel: (514) 842-6111
Fax: (514) 842-9381
Toll free: 1 800 387-3042

Delta Montréal
450, rue Sherbrooke Ouest
Montréal (Québec) H3A 2T4
Metro: Place-des-Arts
Tel: (514) 286-1986
Fax: (514) 284-4342
(guests), (514) 284-4306
(administration)
Toll free: 1 800 268-1133

Hôtel du Parc
3625, avenue du Parc
Montréal (Québec) H2X 3P8
Metro: Place-des-Arts
Tel: (514) 288-6666
Fax: (514) 288-2469
Toll free: 1 800 363-0735
(Canada & U.S.)

Hilton Montréal Bonaventure
1, Place Bonaventure
Montréal (Québec) H5A 1E4
Metro: Bonaventure
Tel: (514) 878-2900
Fax: (514) 878-0028
Toll free: 1 800 267-2575

**Hôtel Inter-Continental
Montréal**
360, rue Saint-Antoine Ouest
Montréal (Québec) H2Y 3X4
Metro: Square-Victoria
Tel: (514) 987-9900
Fax: (514) 987-9904 (admin-
istration), (514) 847-8550
(guests)
Toll free: 1 800 361-3600
Telex: 05-24372

**Hôtel Gouverneur Place
Dupuis**
1415, rue Saint-Hubert
Montréal (Québec) H2L 3Y9
Metro: Berri-UQAM
Tel: (514) 842-4881
Fax: (514) 842-1584
Toll free: 1 888 910-1111

Crowne Plaza Métro Centre
505, rue Sherbrooke Est
Montréal (Québec) H2L 4N3
Metro: Sherbrooke
Tel: (514) 842-8581
Fax: (514) 842-8910
Toll free: 1 800 561-4644
(Canada & U.S.),
1 800 2CROWNE (interna-
tional)

Hôtel Omni Montréal
1050, rue Sherbrooke Ouest
Montréal (Québec) H3A 2R6
Metro: Peel
Tel: (514) 284-1110
Fax: (514) 845-3025
Toll free: 1 800 843-6664

**Hôtel Travelodge Montréal
Centre**
50, boul. René-Lévesque
Ouest
Montréal (Québec) H2Z 1A2
Metro: Place-des-Arts/
Place-d'Armes
Tel: (514) 874-9090
Fax: (514) 874-0907
Toll free: 1 800 578-7878
(U.S. & Canada)

**Holiday Inn Select Montréal
Centre-Ville**
(Downtown/Convention
Centre)
99, avenue Viger Ouest
Montréal (Québec) H2Z 1E9
Metro: Place-d'Armes
Tel: (514) 878-9888

Fax: (514) 878-6341
Toll free: 1 800 HOLIDAY,
1 888 878-9888 (reserva-
tions)

Ritz-Carlton, Montréal
1228, rue Sherbrooke Ouest
Montréal (Québec) H3G 1H6
Metro: Peel
Tel: (514) 842-4212 (guests),
(514) 842-4222 (sales)
Fax: (514) 842-3383
(guests), (514) 842-4907
(sales and banquets),
(514) 842-2268 (reserva-
tions)
Toll free: 1 800 363-0366
(Canada & U.S.)

Hôtel Le Cantlie Suites
1110, rue Sherbrooke Ouest
Montréal (Québec) H3A 1G9
Metro: Peel
Tel: (514) 842-2000
Fax: (514) 844-7808
Toll free: 1 888 Cantlie/
1 800 567-1110

Hôtel Maritime Plaza
1155, rue Guy
Montréal (Québec) H3H 2K5
Metro: Guy-Concordia/
Lucien-L'Allier
Tel: (514) 932-1411 Fax:
(514) 932-0446
Toll free: 1 800 363-6255

**Days Inn Montréal Métro-
Centre**
1005, rue Guy
Montréal (Québec) H3H 2K4
Metro: Lucien-L'Allier/
Guy-Concordia
Tel: (514) 938-4611
Fax: (514) 938-8718
Toll free: 1 800 567-0880

Novotel Montréal Centre
1180, rue de la Montagne
Montréal (Québec) H3G 1Z1
Metro: Peel/Lucien-L'Allier
Tel: (514) 861-6000
Fax: (514) 861-0992
Toll free: 1 800 221-4542/
1 800 NOVOTEL

**Four Points Hôtel & Suites
Sheraton Montréal Centre-
ville**
475, rue Sherbrooke Ouest
Montréal (Québec) H3A 2L9
Tel: (514) 842-3961
Fax: (514) 842-0945
Toll free: 1 800 842-3961

Courtyard Marriott Montréal
410, rue Sherbrooke Ouest
Montréal (Québec) H3A 1B3
Metro: Place-des-Arts
Tel: (514) 844-8855
Fax: (514) 844-0912
Toll free: 1 800 449-6654

**Best Western Europa
Centre-Ville**
1240, rue Drummond
Montréal (Québec) H3G 1V7
Metro: Peel
Tel: (514) 866-6492
Fax: (514) 861-4089
Toll free: 1 800 361-3000

**Château Versailles Hôtel &
Tour**
1659, rue Sherbrooke Ouest,
Montréal (Québec) H3H 1E3
and 1808, rue Sherbrooke
Ouest, Montréal (Québec)
H3H 1E5
Metro: Guy-Concordia
Tel: (514) 933-3611
Fax: (514) 933-6967
Toll free: 1 800 361-7199
(Canada), 1 800 361-3664
(U.S.)

**Best Western Ville-Marie
Hôtel & Suites**
3407, rue Peel
Montréal (Québec) H3A 1W7
Metro: Peel
Tel: (514) 288-4141
Fax: (514) 288-3021
Toll free: 1 800 361-7791

Le Nouvel Hôtel
1740, boul. René-Lévesque
Ouest
Montréal (Québec) H3H 1R3
Metro: Guy-Concordia
Tel: (514) 931-8841
Fax: (514) 931-3233
Toll free: 1 800 363-6063

Hôtel Lord Berri
1199, rue Berri
Montréal (Québec) H2L 4C6
Metro: Berri-UQAM
Tel: (514) 845-9236
Fax: (514) 849-9855
Toll free: 1 888 363-0363

Hôtel Taj Mahal
1600, rue Saint-Hubert
Montréal (Québec) H2L 3Z3
Metro: Berri-UQAM
Tel: (514) 849-3214
Fax: (514) 849-9812

Loews Hôtel Vogue
1425, rue de la Montagne
Montréal (Québec) H3G 1Z3
Metro: Peel
Tel: (514) 285-5555
Fax: (514) 849-8903
Toll free: 1 800 465-6654

Quality Hôtel Centre-ville
3440, avenue du Parc
Montréal (Québec) H2X 2H5
Metro: Place-des-Arts
Tel: (514) 849-1413
Fax: (514) 849-6564
Toll free: 1 800 228-5151

L'Hôtel de la Montagne
1430, rue de la Montagne
Montréal (Québec) H3G 1Z5
Metro: Peel
Tel: (514) 288-5656
Fax: (514) 288-9658
Toll free: 1 800 361-6262

Hôtel du Fort
1390, rue du Fort
Montréal (Québec) H3H 2R7
Metro: Atwater/Georges-Vanier
Tel: (514) 938-8333
Fax: (514) 938-3123
Toll free: 1 800 565-6333

Days Inn Montréal Centre-ville
215, boul. René-Lévesque Est
Montréal (Québec) H2X 1N7
Metro: Saint-Laurent/Champ-de-Mars
Tel: (514) 393-3388
Fax: (514) 395-9999
Toll free:1 800 Days-Inn (329-7466), 1 800 668-3872

Hôtel Comfort Suites
1214, rue Crescent
Montréal (Québec) H3G 2A9
Metro: Lucien-L'Allier/Guy-Concordia
Tel: (514) 878-2711
Fax: (514) 878-0030
Toll free: 1 800 221-2222

Hôtel Le Saint-André
1285, rue Saint-André
Montréal (Québec) H2L 3T1
Metro: Berri-UQAM
Tel: (514) 849-7070
Fax: (514) 849-8167
Toll free: 1 800 265-7071

Hôtel Montréal-Crescent
1366, boul. René-Lévesque Ouest
Montréal (Québec) H3G 1T4
Metro: Lucien-L'Allier
Tel: (514) 938-9797
Fax: (514) 938-9797
Toll free: 1 800 361-5064

Hôtel St-Denis
1254, rue Saint-Denis
Montréal (Québec) H2X 3J6
Metro: Berri-UQAM
Tel: (514) 849-4526
Fax: (514) 849-4529
Toll free: 1 800 363-3364

Hôtel de L'Institut
3535, rue Saint-Denis
Montréal (Québec) H2X 3P1
Metro: Sherbrooke
Tel: (514) 282-5120
Fax: (514) 873-9893
Toll free: 1 800 361-5111 (Quebec only)

Hôtel Bourbon
1574, rue Sainte-Catherine Est
Montréal (Québec) H2L 2J2
Metro: Beaudry
Tel: (514) 523-4679
Fax: (514) 523-1599
Toll free: 1 800 268-4679

Hôtel de Paris
901, rue Sherbrooke Est
Montréal (Québec) H2L 1L3
Metro: Sherbrooke
Tel: (514) 522-6861
Fax: (514) 522-1387

Hôtel du Nouveau Forum
1320, rue Saint-Antoine Ouest
Montréal (Québec) H3C 1C2
Metro: Lucien-L'Allier
Tel: (514) 989-0300
Fax: (514) 931-3090
Toll free: 1 888 989-0300

Hôtel de La Couronne
1029, rue Saint-Denis
Montréal (Québec) H2X 3H9
Metro: Champ-de-Mars/Berri-UQAM
Tel: (514) 845-0901

Hôtel l'Abri du Voyageur
9, rue Sainte-Catherine Ouest
Montréal (Québec) H2X 1Z5
Metro: Saint-Laurent/Place-des-Arts
Tel: (514) 849-2922
Fax.: (514) 499-0151

Auberge des Glycines
819, boul. de Maisonneuve Est
Montréal (Québec) H2L 1Y7
Metro: Berri-UQAM
Tel: (514) 526-5511
Fax: (514) 523-0143
Toll free: 1 800 361-6896

Hôtel Manoir des Alpes
1245, rue Saint-André
Montréal (Québec) H2L 3T1
Metro: Berri-UQAM
Tel: (514) 845-9803
Fax: (514) 845-9886
Toll free: 1 800 465-2929

Auberge Mont-Royal
4544, avenue du Parc
Montréal (Québec) H2V 4E3
Metro: Mont-Royal
Tel: (514) 274-5000
Fax: (514) 274-1414

Hôtel La Résidence du Voyageur
847, rue Sherbrooke Est
Montréal (Québec) H2L 1K6
Metro: Sherbrooke
Tel: (514) 527-9515
Fax: (514) 526-1070

Hôtel Château de l'Argoat
524, rue Sherbrooke Est
Montréal (Québec) H2L 1K1
Metro: Sherbrooke
Tel: (514) 842-2046
Fax: (514) 286-2791

Auberge Le jardin d'Antoine
2024, rue Saint-Denis
Montréal (Québec) H2X 3K7
Metro: Berri-UQAM/
Sherbrooke
Tel: (514) 843-4506
Fax: (514) 281-1491
Toll free: 1 800 361-4506

Hôtel Viger Centre-ville
1001, rue Saint-Hubert
Montréal (Québec) H2L 3Y3
Metro: Berri-UQAM
Tel: (514) 845-6058
Fax: (514) 844-6068
Toll free: 1 800 845-6058,
ext. 599

Hôtel Manoir Sherbrooke
157, rue Sherbrooke Est
Montréal (Québec) H2X 1C7
Metro: Sherbrooke/
Saint-Laurent
Tel: (514) 845-0915
Fax: (514) 284-1126

Manoir Ambrose
3422, rue Stanley
Montréal (Québec) H3A 1R8
Metro: Peel
Tel: (514) 288-6922
Fax: (514) 288-5757
Toll free: 1 800 565-5455,
ext. 115

Auberge de la Fontaine
1301, rue Rachel Est
Montréal (Québec) H2J 2K1
Metro: Mont-Royal
Tel: (514) 597-0166
Fax: (514) 597-0496
Toll free: 1 800 597-0597

Hôtel Casa Bella
264, rue Sherbrooke Ouest
Montréal (Québec) H2X 1X9
Metro: Place-des-Arts
Tel: (514) 849-2777
Fax: (514) 849-3650

Castel St-Denis
2099, rue Saint-Denis
Montréal (Québec) H2X 3K8
Metro: Berri-UQAM/
Sherbrooke
Tel: (514) 842-9719
Fax: (514) 843-8492

Hôtel le Saint-Malo
1455, rue du Fort
Montréal (Québec) H3H 2C2
Metro: Guy-Concordia
Tel: (514) 931-7366
Fax: (514) 931-3764

Hôtel Le Breton
1609, rue Saint-Hubert
Montréal (Québec) H2L 3Z1
Metro: Berri-UQAM
Tel: (514) 524-7273
Fax: (514) 527-7016

Hôtel Villard
307, rue Ontario Est
Montréal (Québec) H2X 1H7
Metro: Berri-UQAM
Tel: (514) 845-9730
Fax: (514) 844-6910
Toll free: 1 800 394-9730

Maison Brunet
1035, rue Saint-Hubert
Montréal (Québec) H2L 3Y3
Metro: Berri-UQAM
Tel: (514) 845-6351
Fax: (514) 848-7061

BED AND BREAKFASTS

Rates are for double occupancy, in high season. Many bed and breakfasts offer discounts in the off-season.

Downtown Central

Le penthouse
1625, boul. de Maisonneuve
Ouest, app. 2609
Montréal H3H 1N4
(514) 933-4399
$75–95

Detour B&B
2267, rue du Souvenir
Montréal H3H 1S3
(514) 934-1564
$60

Au 3438
3438, rue Stanley
Montréal H3A 1R8
(514) 843-5820
$80–90

Auberge Montpetit
3431, rue Aylmer
Montréal H2X 2B4
(514) 845-3984
$24 (single)

Petite Auberge les Bons Matins B&B
1393, rue Argyle
Montréal H3G 1V5
(514) 943-8641
$90–125

Jacky's Bed and Breakfast
3450, rue Drummond, app. 1118A
Montréal H3G 1Y2
(514) 287-1022
$90

Mona Kaufmann
1230, av. Docteur Penfield
Montréal H3G 1B5
(514) 842-3939
$65

Gîte Montréal Centre-Ville
3462, av. Laval
Montréal H2X 3C8
(514) 289-9749
1 800 267-5180
$95

Maison de Bullion
3424, rue de Bullion
Montréal H2X 2Z9
(514) 287-9495
$65

Downtown — West

Le Bosquet Coursol
2251, av. Coursol
Montréal H3J 1C6
(514) 931-1371
$60–95

My House
772, rue Lusignan
Montréal H3C 1Y9
(514) 931-8633
$75

Lola's Bed & Breakfast
4805, boul. de Maisonneuve Ouest
Montréal H3Z 1M4
(514) 937-6454
$45–75

À Bonheur d'Occasion (Happy Times)
846, rue Agnès
Montréal H4C 2P8
(514) 935-5898
$75

Montréal Oasis
3000, rue de Breslay
Montréal H3Y 2G7
(514) 935-2312,
237-4875
$75–80

Downtown — East

À l'Adresse du Centre-Ville
1673, rue Saint-Christophe
Montréal H2L 3W7
(514) 528-9516
$65

Auberge l'Un et l'Autre
1641, rue Amherst
Montréal H2L 3L4
(514) 597-0878
$85–99

Au Git'Ann Bed & Breakfast
1806, rue Saint-Christophe
Montréal H2L 3W8
(514) 525-3938
$35–50

Gîte Sympathique du Centre-Ville
3728, rue Saint-Hubert
Montréal H2L 4A2
(514) 843-9740
$85

Gîte Joel Andriet
2568, rue Joliette
Montréal H1W 3G9
(514) 525-0826
$55–60

Chez Roger Bontemps B&B and Tourist Residences
1441-1445, rue Wolfe
Montréal H2L 3J5
(514) 598-9587
1 888 634-9090
$85–120–240

Gîte Le Chat Bleu
409, rue Saint-Hubert
Montréal H2L 4A8
(514) 527-3421
$67

Daisy's Suites
1599, rue Panet
Montréal H2L 2Z4
(514) 521-5846
$80–90

Gîte B&B du Parc
1308, rue Sherbrooke Est
Montréal H2L 1M2
(514) 528-1308
$95–140

Painpignon
1272, rue Sherbrooke Est
Montréal H2L 1M1
(514) 597-1955
$65

Plateau Mont-Royal

(Hutchison to Iberville & Sherbrooke to Rosemont)

L'Urbain
5039, rue Saint-Urbain
Montréal H2T 2W4
(514) 277-3808
$65–70

Au Roselin de Bagatelle
4534, av. de l'Esplanade
Montréal H2T 2Y5
(514) 499-9585
$60

Maison Grégoire
1764, rue Wolfe
Montréal H2X 2Z9
(514) 524-8086
1 888 524-8086
$185

Gîte de l'Oie Blanche
3490, rue Jeanne-Mance
Montréal H2X 2J8
(514) 282-9861
$70

Gîte Gaétan Breton
3724, rue Jeanne-Mance
Montréal H2X 2K5
(514) 845-4680
$55–65

Studios Jacqueline
3463, rue Sainte-Famille
Montréal H2X 2K7
(514) 845-7711
$80

Gîte du Plateau Mont-Royal
185, rue Sherbrooke Est
Montréal H2X 1C7
(514) 522-3910
$19 (single)

Le Gîte Mariposa
484, rue Prince-Arthur Ouest
Montréal H2X 1T5
(514) 843-7373
$95

Bed & Breakfast de Chez Nous
3717, rue Sainte-Famille
Montréal H2X 2L7
(514) 845-7711
$65–70

Alacoque Bed and Breakfast Revolution
2091, rue Saint-Urbain
Montréal H2X 2N1
(514) 842-0938
Fax: (514) 842-7585
$100

Chambre avec Vue/ Bed and Banana
1225, av. de Bullion
Montréal H2X 2Z3
(514) 878-9843
$55–65

Marmelade Bed and Breakfast
1074, rue Saint-Dominique
Montréal H2X 2W2
(514) 876-3960
$75–100

Chez Pierre et Dominique
271, Carré Saint-Louis
Montréal H2X 1A3
(514) 286-0307
$45–80

Gîte Touristique et Appartements du Centre Ville
3523, rue Jeanne-Mance
Montréal H2X 2K2
(514) 845-0431
$50–75

Chez Alexandre Le Bienheureux
3432, rue Hutchison
Montréal H2X 2G4
(514) 282-3340
$75–85

Castel Durocher
3488, rue Durocher
Montréal H2X 2E1
(514) 282-1697
$85

La Maison Côté
3422, av. Laval
Montréal H2X 3C8
(514) 844-5897
1 800 227-5897
$85–95

Chez Pierre
3600, av. Laval
Montréal H2X 3C9
(514) 284-4226
$49–78

Aux Portes de la Nuit
3496, av. Laval
Montréal H2X 3C8
(514) 848-0833
$80–90

A Bed & Breakfast Downtown Network
3458, av. Laval
Montréal H2X 3C8
(514) 289-9749
1 800 267-5180
$35–95

Angelica Blue Bed and Breakfast
1215, rue Sainte-Élisabeth
Montréal H2X 3C3
(514) 844-5048
$105–120

HOTELS, INNS, BED & BREAKFASTS

Chez Jean
4136, av. Henri-Julien
Montreal H2W 2K3
(514) 843-8279
$17 (single)

Le Zèbre
1281, av. Laval
Montréal H2W 2H8
(514) 844-9868
$65

Welcome Bed and Breakfast
3950, av. Laval
Montréal H2W 2J2
(514) 844-5897
1 800 227-5897
$65–75–85–95

Relais Montréal Hospitalité
2977, av. Laval
Montréal H2W 2H9
(514) 287-9635
1 800 363-9635
$60

Studios du Quartier Latin
2024, rue Saint-Hubert
Montréal H2J 2P8
(514) 840-9144
$55

Le Matou
4420, rue Saint-Denis
Montréal H2J 2L1
(514) 982-0030
$90

Le Cottage Brébeuf
4277, rue Brébeuf
Montréal H2J 3K6
(514) 526-4846
$105 (unit)

Gîte Toujours Dimanche
1131, rue Rachel
Montréal H2J 2J6
(514) 527-2395
$65

Shezelles
4272, rue Berri
Montréal H2J 2P8
(514) 849-8694
Fax: (514) 528-8290
$70–100

Gîte La Cinquième Saison
4396, av. Boyer
Montréal H2J 3E1
(514) 522-6439
$65

Coteau St Louis
5210, rue Berri
Montréal H2J 2S5
(514) 495-1681
$68–72

À la Dormance
4425, rue Saint-Hubert
Montréal H2J 2X1
(514) 529-0179
$50–70

Couette et Café Cherrier
522, rue Cherrier
Montréal H2L 1H3
(514) 982-6848
$55–80

Au Château Cherrier
550, rue Cherrier
Montréal H2L 1H3
(514) 844-0055
$65

Entre Rachel et Marianne
4234, rue de Lorimier
Montréal H2H 2B1
$65

La Pension Vallières
6562 , rue de Lorimier
Montréal H2G 2P6
(514) 729-9552
$60–73

Le Gîte du Parc Lafontaine
1250, rue Sherbrooke Est
Montréal H2L 1M1
(514) 522-3910
$19–43 (single)

Chérie Cherrier B A Guest B&B
422, rue Cherrier
Montréal H2L 2N2
(514) 738-9410
1 800 738-4338
$80

Chagri Bed and Breakfast
1268, rue Sherbrooke Est
Montréal H2L 1M1
(514) 947-1692
$65

Maison Brunet
1035, rue Saint-Hubert
Montréal H2L 3Y3
(514) 845-6351
$64

La Maison Jaune
2017, rue Saint-Hubert
Montréal H2L 3Z6
(514) 524-8851
$55–65

La Maison Cachée
2121, av. Saint-Christophe
Montréal H2L 3X1
(514) 522-4451
$70–80

La Maison du Jardin
3744, rue Saint-André
Montréal H2L 3V7
(514) 598-8862
$60–$85

À la Bonne Étoile
5193, rue de Bordeau
Montréal H2H 2A6
(514) 525-1698
$60

À la Gloire du Matin
4776, rue Parthenais
Montréal H2H 2G7
(514) 523-3019
$60–80

Chez François
4031, av. Papineau
Montréal H2K 4K2
(514) 239-4638
$75–100

Gay Village

Turquoise Bed and Breakfast
1576, rue Alexandre-de-Sève
Montréal H2L 2V7
(514) 523-9943
$70

Le Roi d'Carreau
1637, rue Amherst
Montréal H2L 3L4
(514) 524-2493
$75–105

Les Dauphins
1281, rue Beaudry
Montréal H2L 3E3
(514) 525-1459
$40–65

Douillette et Chocolat
1631, rue Plessis
Montréal H2L 2X6
(514) 523-0162
$65

Ruta Bagage
1345, rue Sainte-Rose
Montréal H2L 2J7
(514) 598-1586
$70

Chambres au Village
850, rue de la Gauchetière Est
Montréal H2L 2N2
(514) 844-6941
$60–70

Old Montreal

Appart-Hôtel du Vieux Montréal
405, rue Saint-Dizier
Montréal H2Y 2Y1
(514) 286-0055
$170–240

Le Gîte Vieux Montréal Bed & Breakfast
209, rue Saint-Paul Ouest, app. 500
Montréal H2Y 2A1
(514) 288-1109
$65

Le Beau Soleil in Old Montréal
355, rue Saint-Paul Est
Montréal H2Y 1H3
(514) 871-0299
$80

Downtown Provincial Bed and Breakfast
206, rue Saint-Paul Ouest, app. 200
Montréal H2Y 1Z9
(514) 285-4060
$55–90

West Island

Ste-Anne Bed & Breakfast
27-A, rue Perrault
Sainte-Anne-de-Bellevue
H9X 2E1
(514) 457-9504
$50–70

Gîte Maison Jacques
4444, rue Paiement
Pierrefonds H9H 2S7
(514) 696-2450
$53–58

Gîte le Vernet
17 703, rue Meloche
Pierrefonds H9J 3R4
(514) 624-6592
$55–75

Les Lorrains
21, 50e Avenue
Lachine H8T 2T4
(514) 634-0884
$60

LaSalle and Verdun

Au Pied des Rapides
96, 2e Avenue
LaSalle H8P 2G2
(514) 366-0024
$55

Chez Edwin et Lucille Mackay
96, 2ᵉ Avenue
LaSalle H8P 2G2
(514) 366-0024
$50–55

Pacane et Potiron Café Couette
1430, av. Rolland
Verdun H4H 2G6
(514) 769-8315
$70–95

Montreal — West End

Carole's Purrfect Bed and Breakfast
3428, rue Addington
Montréal H4A 3G6
(514) 486-3995
$70–75

Overseas Travellers' Club
3497, rue Girouard
Montréal H4A 3C5
(514) 489-9441
$55

Manoir Harvard
4805, av. Harvard
Montréal H3X 3P1
(514) 488-3570
$100–125

Gîte Gilbert
1901, av. Clinton
Montréal H3S 1L2
(514) 342-2179
$45–65

Outremont and Adjacent

Cité Chic Couette & Café
64, av. Nelson
Outremont H2V 3Z7
(514) 279-4659
$95–120

Forest Hill Bed and Breakfast
3210, rue Forest Hill, suite 1406
Montréal H3V 1C7
(514) 738-9410
$50–75

Gîte la Porte des Nuages
823, rue Collard
Montréal H2C 3H8
(514) 272-6346
$65

North and East

Côté Cour, Gîte Urbain
4225, rue Saint-André
Montréal H2J 2Z3
(514) 598-5075
$70–75

Le Clos des Épinettes
1-10358, rue Parthenais
Montréal H2B 2L7
(514) 382-0737
$60

La Maison Peyrot
6822, 25ᵉ Avenue
Montréal H1T 3L9
(514) 721-3010
$60

Chez Monique et Christian B&B
1508, rue Jeanne-d'Arc
Montréal H1W 3T4
(514) 522-2869
$50

B&B Comme Chez-Vous
5105, rue Bélanger
Montréal H1T 1C7
(514) 374-0561
$35–45

Au Gîte Olympique
2752, boul. Pie IX
Montréal H1V 2E9
(514) 254-5423
1 888 254-5423
$75–85

À la Belle Vie
1408, av. Jacques-Lemaistre
Montréal H2M 2C1
(514) 381-5778
$55–60

Le 6400 Couette et Café Bed and Breakfast
6400, rue Lemay
Montréal H1T 2L5
(514) 259-6400
$60–65

Le Petit Bonheur
6790, rue Lemay
Montréal H1T 2L5
(514) 256-3630
$50–65

La Victorienne
12560, rue Notre-Dame Est
Montréal H1B 2Z1
(514) 645-8328
$50

Laval

Via Lavoisier Bed & Breakfast
153, av. Lavoisier
Laval H7N 3J5
(450) 978-7400,
946-5118
$75–140

South Shore

La Villa des Fleurs, Gîte du passant
45, rue Gaudreault
Repentigny J6A 1M3
(450) 654-9209
$50

Au Jardin d'Alexandre
8135, av. Niagara
Brossard J4Y 2G2
(450) 445-2200
$50

Le Relais des îles Percées
85, des Îles-Percées
Boucherville J4B 2P1
(450) 655-3342
$55

Universities, Dormitories and Youth Hostels

Concordia University
7141, rue Sherbrooke Ouest
Montréal H4B 1R6
(514) 848-4757
$22–29

McGill University Residences
3425, rue University
Montréal H3A 2A8
(514) 398-6367
$33

Université de Montréal, service des résidences
2350, boul. Édouard-Montpetit
Montréal H3C 3L7
(514) 343-6531
$23–33

Université du Québec à Montréal
303, boul. René-Lévesque Est
Montréal H2X 3Y3
(514) 987-6669
$33–85

Résidence Lalemant— Collège Brébeuf
5625, av. Decelles
Montréal H3T 1W4
(514) 342-1320
$38

YWCA
1355, boul. René-Lévesque Ouest
Montréal H3G 1T3
(514) 866-9941
$22–55

YMCA (downtown)
1450, rue Stanley
Montréal H3A 2W6
(514) 849-8393
$28–56

Auberge de Jeunesse de L'Hôtel de Paris
901, rue Sherbrooke Est
Montréal H2L 1L3
(514) 522-6861
1 800 567-7217
$17 (single)

Auberge de Jeunesse de L'Hôtel de Paris (Annexe)
874, rue Sherbrooke Est
Montréal H2L 1K9
(514) 522-6861
1 800 567-7217
$17 (single)

Auberge de Jeunesse de Montréal Hostelling International
1030, rue Mackay
Montréal H3G 2H1
(514) 843-3317
$20–60

Résidence du Collège de Bois-de-Boulogne
10 500, av. Bois-de-Boulogne
Montréal H4N 1L4
(514) 332-3008
$22–33

Collège Français
5155, av. de Gaspé
Montréal H2T 2A1
(514) 270-4459
$31–81

Index

Comments—Suggestions

Prices go up, places change ownership and festivals change dates. What was terrific one time of year might be disappointing at another. Sometimes errors simply find their way into the text. Or maybe you have a secret destination you'd like to share with other readers. Whatever the reason, we'd love to hear from you, so don't hesitate to send us your comments or suggestions for improvements.

Write to:
No Fixed Address Publications
P.O. Box 65, NDG Station
Montreal, Quebec
Canada H4A 3P4

e-mail: nfa@cam.org

Ordering a Copy

If you enjoyed *Get Around Town! Montreal* and would like to order a copy directly from the publisher, simply fill out the form below (or a photocopy of it). Travel agents, educators and tour guides, please inquire about volume discounts.

Title	Quantity	Price	Total
Escapades d'un jour, Montréal	_____	$14.95	_____
Get Outta Town! Montreal	_____	$14.95	_____
Escapades en ville, Montréal	_____	$14.95	_____
Get Around Town! Montreal	_____	$14.95	_____
		Subtotal	_____
		GST in Canada 7%	_____
		($1.05 per book)	
		Shipping and handling	Free
Payment: ☐ Money Order ☐ Cheque		Total	_____

Name: _____

Address: _____

City: _____ Province: _____

Country: _____ Postal Code: _____

Signature: _____